exploring a great spiritual practice

pilgrimage

Edward C. Sellner

John Kirvan, series editor

SORIN BOOKS Notre Dame, Indiana

www.avemariapress.com

International Standard Book Number: 1-893732-75-4

Cover and text design by Katherine Robinson Coleman.

Printed and bound in the United States of America.

Library of Congress Cataloging-in-Publication Data

Sellner, Edward Cletus.

Pilgrimage / Edward C. Sellner.

p. cm. — (Exploring a great spiritual practice)

Includes bibliographical references.

ISBN 1-893732-75-4

1. Pilgrims and pilgrimages. I. Title. II. Series.

BL619.P5S45 2004

203′.51—dc22

2004014336

pilgrimage

For Toni Perez,

Jerome Orial,

Pere Mikael,

John Dependahl,

Steve Hegranes,

Bill McCollum,

Matt Lucas,

Chris Narins,

and

Tom Delaney,

COMPANIONS ON THE JOURNEY

"I am haunted by numberless islands, and many a Danaan shore,
Where Time would surely forget us, and
Sorrow come near us no more."

William Butler Yeats, "The White Birds"

"O God, you are the journey
and the journey's end."

Boethius

Contents

exploring a great spiritual practice

Introduction

"We are **pilgrims** on the **earth** and strangers; we have come from **afar** and we are **going far.**"

Vincent van Gogh

This year, like every year, two million devout Moslems will travel to Mecca, Islam's holiest city, to fulfill their religion's demand that everyone who is in good health and has sufficient funds go there at least once in their lifetime.

This year at Varasani in India, on the banks of the Ganges, millions of Hindu and Buddhist followers will bathe in the river's waters hoping to experience physical and spiritual regeneration.

This year five million Christians, also seeking healing and hope, will visit the site in Lourdes, France, near the Spanish border, where the Virgin Mary appeared to a poor peasant girl, Bernadette, in 1858.

This year, too, seven hundred thousand people will travel to Graceland, the home of Elvis Presley, in Memphis, Tennessee, to visit the famous singer's grave, buy t-shirts and badges, and, if they come on the anniversary of his death, participate in a candlelight vigil and procession past the house and the grave.

All of these people from all over the world, representing some of the world's great spiritual traditions, as well as admirers and seekers without any religious affiliation at all, have one thing in common: they are pilgrims. I am one of them.

Since I was a child, seated at my father's side as he delivered gas to the towns of rural Minnesota or next to my mother on my first train ride, I've had a desire to travel, to visit places filled with wonder, to encounter first-hand the landscapes of heroes, wisdom figures, saints. Part of this yearning may have been due to the landscape which I inhabited: that of the Midwest with its flat prairies and endless plains. I know, for certain, that my early love of stories and of books opened up new horizons and a much wider world than the one I physically inhabited. Perhaps too it is genetic, the wanderlust of my Irish and Norman ancestors living in my soul. Whatever the reason, over the past two and a half decades I have gone as a pilgrim to places made holy by those who have taught me with their wisdom and mentored me with their lives. In turn, I have acted as a guide to individuals and to numerous pilgrim groups, believing that when you love something or someone, you naturally want to share that experience with others.

In search of my own spiritual heritage and identity, I have visited the holy sites of the Celtic saints in Ireland, Scotland, Wales, Cornwall, Northumbria, Brittany, and Galicia. My travels have also taken me to Canterbury, England, and Thomas Becket's shrine; to Julian's cell at Norwich where she lived as an anchoress and spiritual guide; to Avila, Segovia, and Manresa in Spain where the great mystics, Teresa, John of the Cross, and Ignatius of Loyola lived and taught; to Russia, the land of tragedy and sorrow which has produced holy guides called *startsi*, holy fools, churches filled with icons (such as the astonishing ones of Andrei Rublev), and breathtaking chanted music; to Einsiedeln, Montserrat, Chartres, and Marseille where the enigmatic Black Madonnas, with the Divine Child in their arms, have smiled so graciously; to Hawaii, the land of spectacular beauty, where East meets West, and where the Blue Buddha in Lahaina spoke to me of peace, serenity, and joy.

Other heroes have invited me to traverse their sacred landscapes. In Oxford, I have knelt in the pew where C. S. Lewis prayed, stood in the pulpit where he preached, and had drinks at the pub where he and his writer-friends, the Inklings, used to meet. In Switzerland, I have visited the gravesite of Carl and Emma Jung in Kusnacht, and pounded on the giant, wooden door at Bollingen, the tower and refuge which the famous psychiatrist built on the shores of Lake Zurich. Closer to home, in New Harmony, Indiana, where the great Lutheran theologian, Paul Tillich, is honored, I have prayed in the open fields of the Roofless Church, contemplated the waters of

Tillich Park, and asked my wife to marry me in the middle of the labyrinth. In the hills of Kentucky, in Thomas Merton's hermitage, I spent a rainy, overcast day reflecting and journaling, inspired by the surroundings of one of my most significant spiritual mentors—while also being tempted throughout the afternoon to steal at least one of his many books (the one on the Celtic Church by Nora Chadwick which I didn't have and which was out-of-print). "Hey, who would know?" a voice kept asking me. I resisted it, eventually taking as a relic only a small, red triangular stone which lay on the ground outside, next to the front door. (A good decision, I might add, since, returning later to the monastery in Brother Patrick Hart's battered pickup truck, Merton's friend and secretary glanced at my briefcase and said, "Can you believe it, people have been known to steal from there?")

I have also traveled to Jerusalem, Rome, and Santiago de Compostela, the three holy cities visited by so many medieval pilgrims. Traversing the Middle East, Jerusalem, Bethlehem, and the Sea of Galilee, in particular, were unforgettable, as well as the Church of the Holy Sepulcher where, when I entered the tomb, my skepticism that this really was where the body of Jesus had lain was turned to reverence and awe by another pilgrim's tears. I had gone to Israel in August (*the* hottest month), following in the footsteps of Jesus, and, like Egeria, the fifth-century Spanish nun and pilgrim who left a record of her journeys. I also crossed the Sinai Desert, visited the Monastery of St. Catherine, and climbed Mount Sinai itself where Moses had received the Ten Commandments. I climbed that holy mountain as a penance for sins against my father who had died suddenly the previous year. It truly was a penance considering the heat and dysentery, not to mention the thousands of steps it took to get to the top—and then to climb down again (safely!). My fellow-pilgrims and I ended our pilgrimage with eucharist at Emmaus, in a church built by the Crusaders, at the site where Jesus, in the blessing and breaking of bread, had made his presence known to two pilgrims he had met on the road.

JoAnne and I first visited Rome on our honeymoon, and once again after our sons were born. On our initial visit we saw the newly-elected Pope John Paul II at an audience in the plaza, and on a later pilgrimage, I participated in a mass in St. Peter's Basilica where I happily caught sight of a familiar figure, St. Patrick, among the other statues looking down at us from the heights above. The catacombs, the churches, and the Coliseum, where Christian martyrs had bravely given up their lives, all spoke to me of the faith and a heritage that had come to me as gift, and which I hoped to pass on to my students and my own sons.

Santiago de Compostela, located in that Celtic part of Spain called Galicia, was one of my most meaningful pilgrimages, taken in the springtime of the year when the vivid colors of blossoming flowers and yellow gorse were just beginning to splash the green countryside. Besides the marvelously carved Portico de la Gloria in the church which contains the glowing face of St. James, the brother of St. John the Evangelist, as well as the wonderfully smiling face of the Hebrew dreamer Daniel (after whom my second son was named), what was so memorable were the tall crosses at numerous crossroads, very similar to those in Brittany, inviting pilgrims to pause, to pray, and to view their stressful lives from a perspective of gratitude.

Other pilgrimages, perhaps more "secular," have taken me to Arlington, Virginia, to stand at the graves of two of my earliest heroes, John and Robert Kennedy; to Springfield, Illinois, to visit Lincoln's home, law office, and tomb; to Auvers-sur-Oise, north of Paris, to see the room where Vincent van Gogh died, and the grave that he shares with his dear brother, Theo. I recalled, while standing in the cemetery, located not far from the church and the wheat fields which he painted, Vincent's words from the first sermon he preached as a seminarian:

> We are pilgrims on the earth and strangers; we have come from afar and we are going far. The journey of our life goes from the loving breast of our Mother on earth to the arms of our Father in heaven. Everything on earth changes; we have no abiding city here; it is the experience of everybody.

Always, I have set off on these journeys with the desire that my travels not only touch my mind, but more importantly my soul. And always, sometimes quite astonishingly, I have experienced moments of synchronicity in which I am helped unexpectedly by strangers, as if I am being led. Sometimes I've discovered that what was to be simply a vacation turned out to be a pilgrimage, an encounter with the sacred, the divine, for example, when I stood silently at Ground Zero in New York or looked into the murky waters in Pearl Harbor where the U.S. Arizona lies, deeply moved by the tragedies that hatred and wars can bring.

This book is about the ancient and contemporary practice of pilgrimage. It is written with the conviction that pilgrimages change us, they touch us at the core; we are not the same when we return to our ordinary lives and daily living. This experience of transformation can happen whether we go halfway around the world or down the block to a local, perhaps neglected, shrine; whether we travel to foreign lands or out into cemeteries where our loved ones rest from their labors. Pilgrims frequently discover at such sites and tombs of heroes, saints, and loved ones what T. S. Eliot expresses poetically in his "Four Quartets":

> . . . You are here to kneel
> Where prayer has been valid. And prayer is more
> Than an order of words, the conscious occupation
> Of the praying mind, or the sound of the voice praying.

> And what the dead had no speech for, when living,
> They can tell you, being dead: the communication
> Of the dead is tongued with fire. . . .

As many pilgrims will attest, there is great value in leaving home, letting go of the familiar, traveling in search of one's identity, roots, true self. "Home is where one starts from," Eliot suggests, but:

> As we grow older
> The world becomes stranger, the pattern more complicated
> Of dead and living.

To leave home and to set forth on a sacred journey with an openness to change is to encounter fire, a symbol of the divine interacting with us in unexpected ways. Pilgrimage, as we will see, is about this meeting of energies, our own and what the universe holds for us, what the American transcendentalist Henry David Thoreau speaks of as "the divine energy everywhere," the fire that can transform our lives.

In the following chapters we will don the pilgrim's hat and take up the pilgrim's staff, traversing sacred landscapes, while also paying attention to the insights of previous generations and traditions other than our own. In chapter one, we will consider some of the dimensions of pilgrimage, and propose certain distinctions between pilgrimage, sightseeing, and vacation. In chapter two, pilgrimage in the great myths and religious traditions which are not Christian will be examined. Chapter three contains a brief look at the rich history of Christian pilgrimage, especially as it relates to desert regions, Celtic Christianity, and medieval life. A common pattern associated with any pilgrim-travels is delineated in chapter four, while chapter five explores common elements of pilgrimage, as well as how to deepen our experiences of it before, during, and after our return.

As pilgrimages have changed me, I hope that you, the reader, will also be transformed, not only by the reading and reflection that you do here, but by your own travels, both externally on pilgrimage and internally with your imagination and your heart. For pilgrimage, especially, is symbolic of the journey of the soul, the desire that lies deep within each of us to embrace and be embraced by the divine spirit, the holy energy, the sacred fire. May your journeys be rich for you, and enriching for those whom you love and serve, for, as Vincent realized in his own brief and tragic life, we are all pilgrims on the earth together; we have come from afar and we are going far on sacred journeys through time, and through eternity.

exploring a great spiritual practice

chapterone

The Practice of Pilgrimage

"When the sweet showers
of April have pierced
The drought of March,
and pierced it to the root . . .
Then people long to go on
pilgrimages."

Chaucer, The Canterbury Tales

Pilgrimage is one of the most ancient practices of humankind. It is associated with a great variety of religions and spiritual traditions. While it can be traced back many centuries to the cultures of Babylonia, Egypt, Greece, and Rome, the pilgrim instinct itself lies deep within the human heart. We are naturally drawn to those places and people who reveal the goodness of God, the beauty of creation, the sacred dimensions of our lives. Like the characters in Chaucer's *Canterbury Tales,* at certain times especially we long to go on pilgrimage. This longing is also expressed by an Irish pilgrim, Celedabhaill, who composed these lines before his departure from Bangor, Ireland, in 926 C.E.:

> It is time for me to pass from the shelter of a habitation,
> To journey as a pilgrim over the waves of the bold and splendid sea. . . .
> Time to deliberate how I may find the great Son of Mary. . . .
> Time to rest, after we have reached the place wherein we may shed our tears.

Sometimes people go on pilgrimage to places that seem entirely foreign to their own traditions or upbringing. Thomas Merton, the twentieth-century Trappist monk and spiritual writer, traveled to Thailand in 1968. Addressing Asian monastic leaders in Bangkok, he said, "I believe that by openness to Buddhism, to Hinduism, and to these great Asian traditions, we stand a wonderful chance of learning more about the potentiality of our own traditions." One of the highlights of Merton's Asian journey was a visit to Polonnaruwa, Sri Lanka, where he saw the seated, standing, and reclining Buddhas. This experience seems to have changed his life. As he wrote in his journal:

> I don't know when in my life I have ever had such a sense of beauty and spiritual validity running together in one aesthetic illumination. Surely with . . . Polonnaruwa my Asian pilgrimage has come clear and purified itself. I mean, I know and have seen what I was obscurely looking for. I don't know what else remains but I have now seen and have pierced through the surface and have got beyond the shadow and the disguise.

Thich Nhat Hanh, a Buddhist monk whom Merton met and referred to affectionately as "my brother," uses a term to describe the transformation that the Trappist monk experienced before the Buddha statues. He speaks of "enlightenment," defining it as "breaking through to the true nature of reality." Thich Nhat Hanh shares Merton's insight into how we can be changed when we travel to foreign shores or unfamiliar places in search of wisdom, healing, or a spiritual awakening. Sometimes our deepest questions are answered by our journeys. But the Buddhist monk, like Merton, also believes in the need to know our own roots first:

> When we respect our blood ancestors and our spiritual ancestors, we feel rooted. If we can find ways to cherish and develop our spiritual heritage, we will avoid the kind of alienation that is destroying society, and we will become whole again. . . . Learning to touch deeply the jewels of our own traditions will allow us to understand and appreciate the values of other traditions, and this will benefit everyone.

Whether a person decides to go in search of his or her own roots or to visit places and sites holy to another, what many contemporary pilgrims, East and West, are experiencing in their travels is an encounter with the past. They have a profound sense of connecting with earlier generations and other times. Early Christian Celts called such holy sites "thin places," places where there seems to be only a thin veil between this world and the next, the finite and infinite, the physical and spiritual realms, the living and the dead. A writer with Celtic origins, Robert Louis Stevenson, alludes to this in his book *Travels to Hawaii:* "There are times and places where the past becomes more vivid than the present, and the memory dominates the ear and eye." For him and the Celts, this perception of the living presence of the past and the awareness of the spiritual dimension to everything is often discovered through an experience of beauty that engenders awe.

Edwin Mullins, in *The Pilgrimage to Santiago* (Interlink Books, 2001), describes how as an atheist he was profoundly affected by the beauty in one of the churches in northern Spain he visited on the road to the shrine of St. James. Stopping at the Benedictine monastery of Santo Domingo de Silos, Mullins discovered a superbly carved panel depicting the journey to Emmaus that two disciples of Jesus undertook following his death. As the scripture story goes, the two men, sad and disappointed, are joined by the resurrected Christ whom they do not recognize. Only when he explains the scriptures to them, how "the Christ should suffer and so enter into his glory," and breaks bread with them, were their eyes opened. He then disappears and they say, "Did not our hearts burn within us as he talked to us on the road?" (cf. Luke 24:13–35).

"Did not our **hearts burn** within us as **he** talked to us on the **road?"**

Luke 24:32

What is interesting about the story is that it posits a relationship between pilgrimage and the heart. What is also amazing about the panel Mullins saw was its portrayal of Christ himself as a pilgrim, carrying a satchel on which is carved a scallop shell, a universal symbol of pilgrimage originally linked with St. James and the pilgrims visiting his shrine at Santiago de Compostela. (It is said that an early Santiago pilgrim who fled to the sea to escape robbers returned to the land covered in shells.) Touched deeply by the beauty of the entire carving, and perhaps the power of the original gospel story itself, Mullins writes:

> That evening, talking with Padre Agustin [his guide], there was no doubt at all in my mind that the cloister of Santo Domingo de Silos was among the most radiantly beautiful places on earth. Should I perhaps have been disturbed by my own very peace of mind? Here was I, after all, an atheist, brought up in tepid C of E [Church of England] and now standing in a Roman Catholic monastery chatting to a monk who referred to my home city of London (albeit chucklingly), as "Babylon," and I dared to experience such a thing as peace of mind.

Mullins' story expresses one of our deepest longings, the need for sacred beauty, beauty that expresses something eternal. The English poet John Keats alludes to this when he writes that "a thing of beauty is a joy forever." A sense of beauty, the discovery of meaning, one's heart being touched—these are experiences often linked with pilgrimage and with some kind of religious or spiritual awakening. Carl Jung equates religious experience with the numinous, that which elicits wonder and awe:

"A thing of **beauty** is a **joy forever.**"

John Keats

> No matter what the world thinks about religious experience, the one who has it possesses a great treasure, a thing that has become for him a source of life, meaning, and beauty, and that has given a new splendor to the world and to mankind. . . . No one can know what the ultimate things are. We must, therefore, take them as we experience them. And if such experience helps to make life healthier, more beautiful, more complete and more satisfactory to yourself and those you love, you may safely say: "This was the grace of God."

Pilgrims are people who may believe or disbelieve all sorts of things, who may identify with a specific religious tradition or not. What unites them, however, is their search for beauty, meaning, or a spiritual dimension to their daily lives. What is ironic perhaps is that sometimes the popularity of pilgrimage rises in direct proportion to lack of regular churchgoing. Shirley du Boulay suggests this in her book on pilgrimage, *The Road to Canterbury:* "It is almost as if pilgrimage becomes even more popular as churchgoing declines; as if pilgrimage meets today's spiritual needs in a way more formal churchgoing does not." This may or may not be so. Certainly there are a lot of churchgoing people who become pilgrims because of their faith, and many pilgrims who find themselves returning more frequently to their own churches precisely because of a pilgrimage they undertook. What is clear, however, is that, despite 9/11 and increased anxieties when we travel, pilgrimage itself is becoming more popular as millions of people throughout the world—Muslims, Jews, Buddhists, Christians, as well as those seekers like Mullins without any specific religious affiliation—set forth as pilgrims each year.

Pilgrimage, Tourism, and Sightseeing

The words "pilgrim" and "pilgrimage" are derived from the Latin *peregrinus* (from *per,* meaning "through," and *ager,* "field" or "land"). A pilgrim is someone who travels beyond his or her known territory (crosses fields) on a journey to new places, landscapes, awarenesses. As the theologian Richard Niebuhr has written, "Pilgrims are persons in motion—passing through territories not their own—seeking something we might call completion or perhaps the word clarity will do as well, a goal to which only the spirit's compass points the way."

> "**Pilgrims** are persons in motion—**passing** through territories not their own—**seeking** something we might call **completion.**"
>
> Richard Niebuhr

Although it is not always easy to distinguish a pilgrim from a tourist or sightseer (sometimes a person's travels can include all these elements), the pilgrim's journey presumes a degree of intentionality. A pilgrim is someone who voyages to a shrine or holy place with the desire for renewal, wisdom, a change of heart. Sightseers go primarily to see new sights, to observe, incorporate, and take home with them an appreciation of a particular location. Many tourists go to escape, relax, or shop. A tourist is often more of a consumer, out to take home what he or she can get. As Anne Tyler's wonderful novel, *The Accidental Tourist* (Penguin, 1998), suggests, such a person sometimes wants to travel from place to place without necessarily being too affected by whom or what he or she encounters.

For pilgrims, however, there is more of focus on their travel as a sacred journey. Pilgrims go to deepen their spirituality, not only for themselves but even for the families they love and the communities to which they belong. If spirituality is about identifying the sacred in one's life and celebrating that relationship to the divine with others, the practice of pilgrimage can contribute to one's spiritual quest. There is in every pilgrim something of the desire, the courage, the hope expressed by Don Quixote in *Man of La Mancha,* when he sings:

To dream the impossible dream,
To fight the unbeatable foe,
To bear with unbearable sorrow,
To run where the brave dare not go.

To right the unrightable wrong,
To love, pure and chaste from afar,
To try, when your arms are too weary,
To reach the unreachable star!

This is my quest, to follow that star,
No matter how hopeless, no matter how far,
To fight for the right, without question or pause,
To be willing to march into hell for a heavenly cause.

And I know, if I'll only be true
To this glorious quest,
That my heart will lie peaceful and calm,

When I'm laid to my rest.
And the world will be better for this,

That one man, scorned and covered with scars,
Still strove, with his last ounce of courage
To reach the unreachable stars!

Whatever other motivations they might have, most pilgrims have at least a latent idealism as well as a willingness, if not outright desire, to be affected by the journey. Glen Grant from Hawaii Tokai International College speaks about the difference between "the accidental tourist" and the "cultural tourist" (the latter term I would associate with being a pilgrim):

> Imagine a visitor to the Hawaiian Island who bypasses sunning on the beautiful beaches and visiting the usual list of tourist attractions. Instead they seek out the hidden Hawaii, the Hawaii teeming with history, culture, ethnicities, and the realities of everyday life both pleasant and discomforting. This visitor believes that the islands have a rich cultural history worth discovering; that neighborhoods contain a fascinating tapestry of heritage worthy of respect. Most important, this visitor is willing to submit to a Hawaiian experience designed to preserve, enhance and perpetuate the deeper community values which are the essence of the world famous "aloha spirit."

Spirit, spirituality: These are primary concerns of pilgrims. Such persons carry with them inner attitudes of openness to the unfamiliar, a desire to be affected by the landscape and the people encountered there, a willingness to experience hardship at times in order to achieve one's goal. But pilgrims also see the journey itself, not just their arrival point, as a sacred enterprise. When it comes to the sacred, pilgrims ask themselves, as did the pilgrims on the road to Emmaus: What evokes reverence, awe, silence, wonder, joy in my heart, or tears of recognition, of gratitude? A person considering becoming a pilgrim can ask the question: Am I setting forth primarily to relax and to simply enjoy another culture, or am I rather looking for an experience that will expand my spirituality, touch my heart? If the ancient Greek term, *metanoia*, translates into "conversion" or "change of heart," then being a pilgrim is about being open to that heart-dimension and the possibility of that transformation of the heart. Pilgrimages, in the widest sense, are journeys with spiritual meaning.

A pilgrim is about being open to that heart-dimension and the possibility of that transformation of the heart.

Travelers can experience their journeys as pilgrimages when they commit themselves to finding something personally sacred on the way. They might also be aware of how important the landscape is that they traverse to get to their destination. While churches and designated holy sites may be particularly significant as places to remember and honor heroes, saints, and loved ones, an awareness of the inherent sacredness of the landscape itself can enrich a pilgrim's journey tremendously. This landscape includes both what is found *on the way* to the holy places, as well as the landscape of the destination. Although I appreciate beautiful churches, when I reach a pilgrimage site I try to imagine the original landscape the saints inhabited rather than the memorials and monuments built there. I remember my amazement on my first journey to Cornwall when I finally reached the holy well of St. Levan, only to find that the few stones left there today (with very little water visible) were much less impressive than the scene *behind the well* of the ocean's blue and green depth, which was lit by the bright rays of the afternoon sun. The saints, I thought then, had a keen eye for beauty; they were no dummies! Often seeking solitude and an ascetic lifestyle, they did not hesitate to choose the most gorgeous, breathtaking sites that appealed to the eye and to the heart.

Sacred Landscape

A recognition that landscape can change a person profoundly is a common idea in the history of the world's spiritual traditions and wisdom figures. Buddha was enlightened while sitting under a banyan tree; Moses encountered God in a burning bush; Muhammad had a vision of the angel Gabriel in a lonely cave outside of Mecca; St. Augustine heard the words of a small child, "take up and read," while in a garden in Milan. None of them were the same after those encounters. If, as the Jewish writer Martin Buber tells us, "all real living is meeting," this meeting definitely includes the environment in which we were raised or live. "Tell me the landscape in which you live, and I will tell you who you are," wrote the Spanish philosopher José Ortega y Gasset. This meeting includes the places we visit.

Each of us is affected deeply by geography and landscape. The naturalist writer, Henry Beston, in *The Outermost House,* tells of his experience living a solitary year on Cape Cod. He had initially planned on spending just two weeks in his house on the shore but then became possessed by the "beauty and mystery of this earth and outer sea." Observing the rhythms of nature and the recurring cycles of the year, he describes what he calls "the pilgrimages of the sun" across the sky, and at night, strolling the beach, "the dust of stars" that fill "the night sky in all its divinity of beauty." "For a moment of night," he writes, "we have a glimpse of ourselves and of our world islanded in its stream of stars—pilgrims of mortality, voyaging between horizons across eternal seas of space and time." "Nature," he continues, "is a part of our humanity, and without some awareness and experience of that divine mystery man ceases to be man." Beston suggests that we especially pay attention not only to the landscape of nature, but to its *sounds* as well:

> The three great elemental sounds in nature are the sound of the rain, the sound of wind in a primeval wood, and the sound of outer ocean on a beach. I have heard them all, and of the three elemental voices, that of ocean is the most awesome, beautiful, and varied. . . . The sea has many voices.

With awareness of one's outer landscape and attention to its sights and sounds, a person can—no matter where one's pilgrimage leads—begin to experience what Beston calls "the old loveliness of earth which both affirms and heals." His pilgrimage to the Cape had been preceded by another to Spain, which he recalls as he observes a blue wave rolling in "out of the blue spaciousness of sea":

"The old loveliness of **earth** which both affirms and **heals.**"

Henry Beston

> On the other side of the world, just opposite the Cape, lies the ancient Spanish province of Galicia, and the town of Pontevedra and St. James Compostela, renowned of pilgrims. (When I was there they offered me a silver cockle shell, but I would have none of it, and got myself a sea shell from some Galician fisherfolk.)

Besides that outer vista, there is the inner landscape of the soul, what Jung terms our "ancestral memories," that lead us in certain directions and perhaps down unexplored paths. Hence, sometimes when we first visit a pilgrimage site, there may be an experience of *déjà vu*, of having been there before. Past lives? Possibly, but more probably our sense of *déjà vu* is related to the past landscapes of our ancestors, memories passed on to us that we only vaguely remember. Dreams sometimes open up that door, as do our visits to foreign shores. The first time I visited Ireland, the home of my ancestors, and walked the hills around Glendalough, the site of an early Celtic monastic community, I felt as if I had been there before. In the crowded streets of Dublin, I heard my Irish grandmother's voice in the voices of the older women whom I encountered; I saw her face in their faces. Other people I have met over the years have related similar experiences that happened to them when first visiting the home of their ancestors. There is within us a link, conscious and unconscious, with other landscapes, other generations, other times.

To be **rooted** is perhaps one of the most **important** and least recognized needs of the **human soul.**

Experiences of place and space affect our identity and our relationship with the divine. To be rooted is perhaps one of the most important and least recognized needs of the human soul.

Spirituality is tied to an awareness and an appreciation of our roots. Spirituality is also linked to the particular place where one receives a new angle of vision. All of us carry in our minds a list of places that are sacred to us. The irony, it seems, is that we frequently have to leave home to find our roots, our identity.

A Sense of Presence

Besides the landscape, other expressions of "meeting" or encounter are the graves or tombs of our ancestors, familial and spiritual. The scholar Peter Brown reminds us that medieval Christian pilgrims were "not merely going to a place; they were going to a place to meet a person." An inscription on the tomb of Martin of Tours, the saint who gave half of his cloak to a poor man only to discover later in a dream that the man was Christ himself, acknowledges this belief:

> Here lies Martin the bishop, of holy memory,
> Whose soul is in the hand of God's, but he is fully here,
> present and made plain in miracles of every kind.

Ancient people, including the Celts, Norse, and Native Americans, believed that to sleep on or near the graves of one's ancestors was to be given special wisdom, which sometimes would be manifested in a dream. Later Christian saints endorsed that belief by traveling to the shrines of their own saintly heroes. In the early seventh century, St. Columbanus, Irish missionary to the European continent, slept overnight at the tomb of St. Martin, praying for guidance before continuing his work. In the sixteenth century, St. Ignatius of Loyola spent the eve of the feast of the Virgin Mary at Montserrat in Spain at the shrine of the Black Madonna, sometimes kneeling before the altar, he says in his autobiography, and "at other times standing, with his pilgrim's staff in his hand."

Russian Orthodox Christians, with their long tradition of pilgrimage, also affirm the value of this practice. One of their most beloved nineteenth-century saints, St. Seraphim of Sarov, explicitly expresses this belief:

> When I am no longer with you, come to my tomb often, bring all your worries, all your troubles, tell me everything that is grieving you, talk to me as to a living person because, for you, I shall go on living; I shall listen to you and your sorrow will disappear.

The writer Andrew Harvey, an atheist, in his autobiography *Hidden Journey: A Spiritual Awakening* (Penguin, 1992), describes his own experience of enlightenment at the tomb of Aurobindo, an Indian holy man. At the age of twenty-five, after studying at Oxford University in England, Harvey decided to return to his native India. He wrote:

Slowly Jean-Marc [his friend] persuaded me to go with him to the ashram to visit Aurobindo's tomb, to examine my earlier dismissal of meditation. One day he said, "Why don't you just sit by Aurobindo's tomb and see what happens?" I sat day after day with the other meditators by the white slab heaped with lotuses and jasmine. Nothing happened; I just felt hot, sad, and angry at the confusion in my mind. Then, one afternoon, just as I had decided to leave and get some tea, the thoughts that had been racing through my brain were suddenly silenced. I felt my entire being gasp for joy, a kind of joy I had never before experienced. I did not tell Jean-Marc for fear that if I talked about the experience it would vanish—but it repeated with more or less the same intensity for days afterward. At last I told him.

"When I am **no longer with you,** come to my tomb often, bring all your worries, all your troubles, tell me everything that is grieving you, **talk to me** as to a living person because, for you, I shall go on living; I shall listen to you and your **sorrow** will **disappear.**"

St. Seraphim of Sarov

"Well . . . ," Jean-Marc smiled. . . . "Your new life is starting."

Visiting the tombs of saints and wisdom figures was and is a holy venture, for these sites may provide a location for the healing, forgiving, and guiding powers of God. When we go there, we frequently find a surprising sense of presence, as if these spiritual mentors are still very much alive and more than willing to be of help. If we visit the graves of our departed loved ones, we might have a similar experience. My friend Jim told me of the time when he was a young man in college and went to the grave of his father, who had died suddenly when Jim was fourteen. He had gone there because he wanted to make a connection with his father and seek some guidance about what to do with his life. He wanted to make his father proud by doing the right thing, but wasn't sure what that right thing was. Talking there at the grave, Jim said he came away with a sense of being heard and helped. My mother-in-law tells how every Sunday she went with her mother and grandmother to visit the grave of her grandfather. This was a custom that many people besides her own family participated in on a weekly basis. They communed with the dead on Sunday afternoons and then went to the local church for Benediction. They felt part of a spiritual community that transcends death itself.

Similar beliefs and practices exist in traditions other than Christianity. When I was in the Sinai desert, I came across at least two hundred Bedouins who were gathering at the tombs of their grandparents. They pitched their tents at an oasis near the graves. They told me that they did this every year for a week or two. It strengthened their familial and tribal ties because they shared meals together, and it gave their children a chance to hear the stories of their ancestors. Muslims travel to Mecca, where they believe that Abraham and his son Ishmael were the first pilgrims, and to Medina, where the prophet Muhammad began his own "Farewell Pilgrimage." Many Buddhists visit the small town in India of Bodhgaya, where the Buddha received enlightenment. They believe that when a pilgrim does this, she or he will never be reborn in one of the lower states of existence, just because of the power of the place. Meanwhile Hindus can visit the sites in India associated with the life of Krishna: his birthplace, a tree by the river where he hung his clothes, a grove where he danced in the middle of the night. Such places are said to bear the "traces" of Krishna.

On a perhaps less religious note, but no less significant spiritually, Phil Cousineau in *The Art of Pilgrimage* tells the story of Brenda Knight, a Chaucerian scholar and author who moved to San Francisco from New York in the late 1980s. Shortly after her arrival, she went to City Lights Bookstore, which is associated with the writers of the Beat Generation, whom she loved. One night she consulted her Tarot cards and up came the Fool, the card of the pilgrim. This confirmed for her the need to return to New York, the place where the Beats had begun. "How else," she asked herself, "are you going to know about them unless you go?" Back in New York, she visited all the haunts of Allen Ginsberg, and all the places that Pollock, Corso, Jannine Pommie Vega, and Jack Kerouac had hung out. "There was an air of desperation," she acknowledged, "but I felt I had made a mysterious connection with them. I kept up my research, especially into Kerouac. He was truly the one. I believed there was some kind of fate that drew us together. Walking in his footsteps through Greenwich Village was like going to the Holy of Holies—you don't need to go to church if you can go to the source of great literature. . . . What better way to understand the secret of a writer's creativity than to walk in their path?" This pilgrimage proved quite valuable to her book, *Women of the Beat Generation* (Conari Press, 1996).

To go on pilgrimage, then, is to set forth in search of what is or what might be sacred to us. It may be the search for our own religious or family history. It may reflect a person's passions for music, art, architecture, books, nature, or food. Through encounters with the landscape and with ancestors, saints, wisdom figures, heroes, mentors, and guides, a pilgrim can begin to clarify his or her identity, and on a deeper level, her or his authentic Self. Such encounters elicit from us sacred stories, holy memories, and new, perhaps deeper wells of spiritual energy we can draw from. On the journey, we may discover our hearts strangely touched, like the two on the road to Emmaus when they encountered the living presence of Christ. Upon our return, we might also come to see that the journey was its own reward.

"To set out boldly in our work is to make a pilgrimage of our labors, to understand that the consummation of work lies not only in what we have done, but who we have become while accomplishing the task."

David Whyte

exploring a great spiritual practice

chapter**two**

Ancient Stories and Traditions

"Leave your country, your family and your father's house, for the land I will show you."

Genesis 12:1–2

"He who leaves home in search of wisdom walks in the path of God."

Muhammad

"You cannot travel the path until you have become the path."

Gautama Buddha

From our earliest days, people have made sacred journeys seeking wisdom, healing, guidance, and inspiration. The Bible and the Quran, as well as the holy texts of Buddhism and Hinduism, encourage their followers to travel to the lands of their founders and to the tombs of their saints. The earliest recorded pilgrim is Abraham, who is revered by the three great monotheistic religions: Judaism, Christianity, and Islam. At the age of 75, Abraham with his courageous wife Sarai left Ur in Mesopotamia four thousand years ago, following God's call: "Leave your country, your family and your father's house, for the land I will show you. I will make you a great nation" (Gn 12:1–2). He became a paradigmatic figure for many later pilgrims who, while they feared the hardships ahead, set forth on a journey with faith.

Another ancient story, the *Epic of Gilgamesh*, was written more than 3700 years ago in Babylonia (present-day Iraq). It tells of the friendship between Gilgamesh, the handsome king of Uruk, and his "mirror image," Enkidu, a man raised in the wilderness who ran with animals. While the storyteller depicts the two men as extremely different in social terms, each brings to the other a gift of wholeness that would not have been experienced except for each other's love. When Enkidu dies suddenly, Gilgamesh, shocked and grieving intensely, goes in search of his ancestor, Utanapishti. He hopes to learn "the secret" of death and life. His is a journey to find meaning in the face of the death. When he finally encounters his ancestor, he is told that death is inevitable for every living creature, and that he should accept his own and his friend's mortality, and return to Uruk to rule more wisely than he had done before. The epic ends with Gilgamesh's return. He is transformed by his loss and the journey of grief it entailed, and aware that "wherever I turn, there too will be Death," but also aware that in the shadow of death he must seek life.

Homer, who died about 700 B.C.E., gives another account. *The Odyssey* is about the adventures of Odysseus, a Greek hero who sets sail for his homeland after ten years of fighting the Trojan War. His story relates "many the pains he suffered in his spirit on the wide sea, struggling for his own life and the homecoming of his companions." He finally reaches his island home in Ithaca and his beloved wife and son. Although perhaps not a pilgrimage in any conventional sense, this is an archetypal myth of journey and return. It contains many of the themes of pilgrimage, such as the sense of a difficult passage fraught with suffering and the intense yearning for a distant goal. The same can be said of the Roman poet Virgil's classic, the *Aeneid*, written between 30–19 B.C.E., describing Aeneas, a Trojan hero, who flees Troy, carrying his father on his back. After years of wandering in search of a new home and falling in love with Dido, the queen of Carthage, he eventually is instrumental in founding Rome. In ancient allegorical tradition, Homer's and Virgil's stories were highly symbolic of the inner spiritual journey everyone must take to find his or her authentic home.

Pilgrim Rituals and Early Practices

The great epics of the ancient world describe various forms of pilgrimage. Many cultures also developed their own pilgrimage rituals and practices. In Greece, for example, after the construction of the Acropolis in Athens in the fourth century B.C.E., one of the principal festivals, the Great Panathenaea, brought thousands of Greeks to the city every four years to celebrate the birthday of the goddess Athena. The statue of Athena, dressed in flowing robes, was undressed, washed, and redressed at different events. There were processions with horsemen and chariots, bearers of offerings, sacrificial animals, and women carrying ritual objects.

Other ancient pilgrims traveled to places of special power or numinosity, such as the Parthenon in Athens or to Delphi, the sacred Greek center of divination, prophecy, and healing.

These locations were decorated with works of art: carvings, paintings, and images that probably amazed those who journeyed there. People were moved by the combination of both aesthetic and religious beauty.

Pilgrims to the temple at Delphi frequently slept overnight inside the shrine, hoping for a vision or a dream to guide them or for some miraculous healing to occur. This practice of paying attention to dreams was taken seriously by ancient peoples, including the Jews who depict some their great heroes, Jacob (Gn 28:10–22), Joseph (Gn 40–41), and Daniel as being dreamers and dream-interpreters. At many of the Greek and Roman sites, pilgrims left prayer petitions, sometimes in the form of curses, and returned to leave gifts as an expression of gratitude when prayers were answered. Remnants of these customs can still be seen at the thermal waters of Bath, England. When Christianity became legitimized in the fourth century by the sympathetic Roman emperor Constantine, some of these same practices were inaugurated. Rather than visiting the sites of the gods and goddesses, Christians now lit candles or left offerings at the churches and shrines dedicated to Jesus, his mother, Mary, and the saints.

Pilgrims in the ancient world also frequently prepared spiritually for a pilgrimage they were about to undertake. In Roman times, one anonymous pilgrim to the shrine at Talmis in Egypt wrote, "I made myself a stranger to all vice and all godlessness, was chaste for a considerable period, and offered the due incense offering in holy piety." Later Christian pilgrims also prepared for their travels through spiritual practices, including confessing to a priest before their departure and fasting along the way. Many Islamic and Buddhist pilgrims still fast, abstain from alcohol and sex, and pray fervently before beginning and while on their pilgrim trips.

Jewish Pilgrimage

The Hebrew people have a long history of pilgrimage. It is rooted in the stories of Abraham and Moses. As people often displaced and persecuted, they feel a special responsibility to follow the practices of their ancestors. We have already looked at Abraham; now we turn to Moses. The story of the Exodus relates how Moses led his people out of Egypt. They wandered through the wilderness for forty years and eventually arrived in the promised land. Even then, this sense of homecoming was short-lived. In the sixth century B.C.E., following the destruction of Solomon's Temple by Nebuchadnezzar in 586, the Jews were exiled to Babylon; in 70 C.E., after the destruction of the temple by the Roman emperor Titus, they were sent into exile once again. Not until the creation of the modern state of Israel in 1948 did they finally begin to experience some degree of relief. Thus, the themes of exile, lamentation, and yearning for the promised land are central to their history and spirituality, perhaps best expressed in the first six verses of Psalm 137:

> Beside the streams of Babylon
> we sat and wept
> at the memory of Zion,
> leaving our harps
> hanging on the poplars there.
> For we had been asked
> to sing to our captors,
> to entertain those who had carried us off:
> "Sing," they said
> "some hymns of Zion."
> How could we sing
> one of Yahweh's hymns
> in a pagan country?
> Jerusalem, if I forget you,
> may my right hand wither!
> May I never speak again,
> if I forget you!
> If I do not count Jerusalem
> the greatest of my joys!

In remembrance of their years of wandering and diaspora, Jewish rituals developed to help participants recall their history of suffering and survival. The key feast of Passover celebrates the beginning of the Exodus, while Sukkot, the Feast of Tabernacles, memorializes the temporary dwellings in which the Israelites lived while wandering in the Sinai wilderness.

> **"Take off your shoes, for the place on which you stand is holy ground."**
>
> *Exodus 3:5–6*

With their faith in one, holy, and all-powerful God (in contrast to the prevailing polytheism of antiquity), the Jews believed that Yahweh could not be confined to any one geographical location. Still, they eventually came to believe that some sites were particularly holy because they were associated in a special way with God's presence. On Mount Sinai Moses was admonished by God, "Take off your shoes, for the place on which you stand is holy ground" (Ex 3:5–6), and the description of the theophany (Ex 19:16–19) on that holy mountain pulses with numinosity:

> Now at daybreak on the third day there were peals of thunder on the mountain and lightning flashes, a dense cloud, and a loud trumpet blast, and inside the camp all the people trembled. Then Moses led the people out of the camp to meet God; and they stood at the bottom of the mountain. The mountain of Sinai was entirely wrapped in smoke, because Yahweh had descended on

> it in the form of fire. Like smoke from a furnace t' smoke went up, and the whole mountain shook violently.

Not only, then, did Mount Sinai come to be seen as a holy place, but also, as Psalm 137 suggests, the city of Jerusalem, the site of the Temple of God. This was *the* city to which the Jewish people would go each year to celebrate the Passover and to offer sacrifices. After the temple's destruction, Jerusalem became the pilgrimage site to which Jews in the diaspora journeyed. One pilgrim in the Middle Ages, a Rabbi Benjamin of Tudela, left an account of his travels from his home in Spain in the 1160s to Italy, Greece, Constantinople, through the Middle East to Jerusalem and Palestine. His main objective was to visit the Jewish communities in the territories ruled by Christians and Muslims, but he also had a special interest in visiting Jewish sacred sites. He writes on one occasion:

> Mount Carmel. Under the mountain are many Jewish sepulchers, and near the summit is the cavern of Elijah, upon whom be peace. Two Christians have built a place of worship near this site, which they call St. Elias. On the summit of the hill you may still trace the site of the altar which was rebuilt by Elijah of blessed memory.

Anticipating contemporary Jewish pilgrims, he also describes the Jews in Jerusalem as going to the Western Wall (called the Wailing Wall today) to pray: "the Western Wall, one of the walls which formed the Holy of Holies of the ancient Temple; it is called the Gate of Mercy, and all Jews resort thither to say their prayers near the wall of the courtyard."

What Rabbi Benjamin's journal suggests is that aside from Jerusalem, other sites were also being visited which were linked with the heroes of Judaism. Jerusalem maintained its primacy for Jewish pilgrims, as it would for Christians and Muslims as well. But increasingly, from late antiquity through medieval to modern times, pilgrimage to the tombs of religious ancestors occurred, whether they were located in Jerusalem or not. The grave of Ezekiel, for example, at Dhu'l-Kifl, was sacred not only to Jews but Muslims too, for whom the prophet was considered a saint. Many of the Jewish holy places were also visited by Christian pilgrims to Palestine, such as those described in the writing of St. Jerome or the Spanish nun, Egeria, as we will see.

Jews today continue their ancient spiritual tradition. They may visit Israel, the land of their ancestors, and gather at the Wailing Wall in Jerusalem to pray. Or they may travel to sites honoring the victims of the Nazi Holocaust, such as those in

Washington, D.C., Poland, or Jerusalem. One of the most visited sites is the Synagogue at the Hadassah Medical Centre in Jerusalem, where the stained-glass windows of the Russian Jewish artist Marc Chagall depict in beautiful, vivid colors the twelve tribes of Israel, a people whom God "brought out of the land of Egypt, out of the house of slavery" (Ex 20:1–2).

Islam and its Hajj

Pilgrimage, called by Muslims *hajj*, is one of their five "Pillars of Faith." These tenets define and direct the daily living and spirituality of Muslims. In addition to bearing witness, praying (at least five times a day), fasting, and giving alms, they are required (if financially and physically able) to make at least one visit during their lifetime to the shrine of the Ka'ba at Mecca, located in Saudi Arabia. The Quran states: "Pilgrimage to the House is incumbent upon men for the sake of Allah, upon every one who is able to undertake the journey to it" (Quran, III:97). Today, as many as two million Muslim pilgrims gather at Mecca for ten days each year to commemorate key events from the founding of Islam and from the time of Abraham.

Islam was founded by the prophet Muhammad in the seventh century when he was living in Mecca and nearby Medina. Through the archangel Gabriel he received a revelation from God; it was recorded by his followers in the Quran, "the

Today, as many as two million Muslim pilgrims gather at Mecca for ten days each year to commemorate key events from the founding of Islam and from the time of Abraham.

Perfect Book." This sacred writing helped define the new religion that eventually united the diverse Arab tribes, with their polytheistic beliefs, into one of the most powerful monotheistic religions in the world. Its beliefs draw upon earlier Jewish and Christian traditions and scriptures. Islam means "submission" to God (Allah) or "the joy that comes through surrender."

The *hajj* is to be performed between the eighth and thirteenth days of the twelfth month of the Muslim year. According to Islamic custom, pilgrims need to wear prescribed white clothing called *ihram* and adopt certain spiritual practices: "The pilgrimage is performed in the well-known months; so whoever determines the performance of the pilgrimage, there shall be no intercourse nor fornication nor quarrelling amongst one another; and whatever good you do, Allah knows it" (Quran, II:197). From the time the pilgrim puts on the white clothing until the completion of the pilgrimage, he or she is to pray for forgiveness and enlightenment, and be devoted to *dhikr*, which means the constant repetition of the prayer, "There is no divinity but Allah."

The purpose a pilgrim's travel to Mecca is to see the Ka'ba, a small building draped in black. It is surrounded by a large courtyard that allows thousands of pilgrims to walk around it in concentric circles and pray for purity of heart. (Unfortunately, occasionally hundreds are killed when a stampede occurs.) Inside the Ka'ba is the famous black stone (perhaps a meteorite), embedded in a wall about two feet from the ground. Some Muslims believe this stone is a relic from Adam or Abraham; some think that it was sent by an angel of Allah. Whatever its origins, most believe that it was kissed by Muhammad himself. The object of each pilgrim is to kiss it too, and part of the stone over the centuries has been worn down by the kisses of these pilgrims. Once the Islamic pilgrim has kissed this stone and walked around the building seven times, other rituals and holy sites follow, including a journey to the Mount of Mercy at Arafat, a site about twelve miles east, where Muhammad is said to have addressed his followers for the last time. Later a sheep or other animal is ritually slaughtered, with the injunction to the pilgrim, before

returning home, to "feed the needy, those who are content and those who are distressed" (Quran, 22).

Ibn Battuta, a theologian born in Tangier in 1304, went on so many pilgrimages in his life to Islamic holy places that he became known as the "Traveler of Islam."

Over the centuries, pilgrimage to other places besides Mecca or Medina developed. Some journeys were for scholarly reasons. Others followed the dictates of Muhammad, who had said, "He who leaves home in search of wisdom walks in the path of God." Pilgrims visited tombs of the Shi'ite martyrs and Muslim mystics, called Sufis. As Muhammad al-Kittani, an Islamic scholar, wrote in the late nineteenth century, "Without saints the sky would not send rain, the earth would not cause its plants to grow, and calamity would pour upon the inhabitants of the earth." Ibn Battuta, a theologian born in Tangier in 1304, went on so many pilgrimages in his life to Islamic holy places that he became known as the "Traveler of Islam." He journeyed across Asia and Africa, visiting and praying at holy sites, but kept returning to Mecca. He writes of his early experiences:

> I set out alone, finding no companion to cheer the way with friendly intercourse. . . . Swayed by an overmastering impulse within me, and a long-cherished desire to visit those glorious sanctuaries, I resolved to quit all my friends and tear myself away from home. As my parents were still alive, it weighed grievously upon me to part from them, and both they and I were afflicted with sorrow.

When he tells of his pilgrimage to Jerusalem, his words convey a Muslim's reverence for that place: "We then reached Jerusalem (may God ennoble her!), third in excellence after the two holy shrines of Mecca and Medina, and the place whence the Prophet was caught up into heaven." One can still see today the mosque called the Dome of the Rock, built where Judaism's temple had once stood, the footprints in stone from where Muhammad is said to have bodily ascended.

Islam is the religious tradition that seems to value pilgrimage the most.

Islam is the religious tradition that seems to value pilgrimage the most. Yet there are those who warn against putting too much stock in the practice alone. Sufi Abu Sa'id, born in 967 C.E., recommended that his followers avoid the *hajj* in order to concentrate on their mystical experiences. When asked why he had not gone to Mecca, he said, "Why have I not performed the Pilgrimage? It is no great matter that you should walk a thousand miles in order to visit a stone house. The true man of God sits where he is, and the Bayt al-Ma'Mur (the celestial Ka'ba) comes several times in a day and night to visit him and performs the circumambulation above his head. Look and see!" Among the Muslims of India, the Sufi mystic Shaykh Nizam ad-din Awliya warned his followers against "pilgrims who, on their return from Arabia, speak of nothing but the pilgrimage. They talk about it incessantly on every occasion. This is not proper." Then he went on: "Somebody used to say, 'I have visited such-and-such a place, and I have seen such-and-such a holy person there.'" Another person asked the mystic, "What good has this been?" and the Shaykh replied, "Clearly no benefit has come from it; that is to say, he is still the egotist he was before!"

"The heart of the believer is the sanctuary of God, and nothing but God is allowed access there."

Prophet Muhammad

Sufis generally valued the workings of the heart over the practice of pilgrimage. They remembered the words of the Prophet Muhammad: "The heart of the believer is the sanctuary of God, and nothing but God is allowed access there." One of the most famous Sufis, Jelalludin Rumi, who lived in the thirteenth century, refers to the origins of the spiritual quest with his evocative phrase, "Anyone pulled from the source wants to go back." He says:

> The heart's the only house of safety, my friends;
> It has fountains, and rose gardens within rose gardens.
> Turn to the heart and go forward, travelers of the night;
> There's where you'll find trees and streams of Living Water.

And in another poem, he speaks more specifically about pilgrimage:

> You went on pilgrimage to Mecca, but where are you now?
> Come, come; here is where you find the Beloved.
> Your Beloved's your nearest neighbor.

Another Sufi poet, Abdallah al-Ansari, writing in the eleventh century, refers to the importance of inner change:

> Know that God Most High has built an outward
> Ka'ba out of mud and stone,
> And fashioned an inward Ka'ba of heart and soul alone.
> The outward Ka'ba, Abraham did build,
> The inward Ka'ba was as the Lord Almighty willed.

Hinduism and Buddhism

Two other great spiritual traditions that count millions as followers have their origins in India. Both traditions see the value of pilgrimage as a spiritual resource and encourage their people to go on pilgrimage if they can.

Hinduism traces some of its spiritual themes and forms to the third millennium B.C.E. It does not look back to a single religious founder or a decisive historical event that brought it into being. Hinduism has many gods and goddesses who all originate from an original creative force called Brahma. Each god and goddess represents a different divine aspect. For example, Shiva is known as "the destroyer," Vishnu is "the preserver," and Krishna is the god of love. Numerous Hindu holy sites are linked to the landscape, such as hilltops, caves, rock mounds, forests, and junctures of rivers. Like the ancient Irish, many Hindus believe the very soil is the body or residence of the divine, particularly in its female form. Again, like the ancient Celtic race, many of the sites visited by Hindu pilgrims are centers of goddess worship.

Water and the feminine are often linked symbolically, and much of Hindu pilgrimage is equated with bodies of water and ceremonial bathing. The Sanskrit term for pilgrimage is *tirthayatra*; *yatra* means the act of travelling, and *tirtha* refers to running water and ritual bathing. In India, there are seven rivers considered particularly holy, of which the Ganges (referred to as "the flowing ladder to heaven") is the most respected. Bathing in the Ganges River, in fact, is the most famous pilgrimage practice in all of India. The Hindu scriptures, the Vedas, explicitly tell of journeys to sacred river fords. To be a Hindu pilgrim is to desire purification, the washing of one's sins away, as the sacred texts reveal:

> Flower-like the heels of the wanderer,
> His body grows and is fruitful;
> All his sins disappear,
> Slain by the toil of his journeying.

The great Hindu epic, the *Mahabharata*, recommends a form of wandering to a wide variety of holy places, but the most important journey is the journey inward. The *Mahabharata* refers to the "*tirthas* of the heart," suggesting that the pilgrim should not only bathe in the waters of earthly *tirthas*, but especially the inner virtues of truth, love, patience, and self-control. Pilgrimage is associated with a certain asceticism, such as fasting, celibacy, the rejection of soft beds and other comforts. A counterpoint, a bit satirical, is offered by Kabir, a great medieval Hindu poet who seems to want to put Hindu pilgrimage into perspective:

> Going on endless pilgrimage, the world died,
> exhausted by so much bathing!

Although substantial Hindu communities exist today in Europe, Africa, and North America, the vast majority of Hindus live in the modern nation of India. Because they worship a great variety of gods and goddesses, there is a tremendous diversity of festivals, feasts, and pilgrimages.

The second great religious tradition to come out of India is Buddhism. Its founder was Prince Siddhartha Gautama (563–483 B.C.E.), who became known as the Buddha or "Enlightened One" following an experience of transformation under a bodhi or banyan tree. Before his death, he recommended to his followers that they undertake pilgrimages to four places in northern India associated with his life: the first, where he was born (perhaps modern Rummindei in Nepal); the second, where he attained enlightenment (Bodhgaya); the third, where he preached his first sermon (the deer park at Sarnath near Benares); and the fourth, where he would die and enter his final nirvana (at Kushinagar). Buddha said that anyone who dies "while making the pilgrimage to these shrines with a devout heart will, at the breaking up of the body after death, be reborn in a heavenly world." He also told them *not* to focus their attention on his bodily remains, an admonition that some have followed and many have not. Sri Lanka, for example, has a famous shrine that supposedly has a tooth of the Buddha, while another site, Rangoon Burma's Schwe Dagon Pagoda, is said to contain some of the Buddha's hairs. Nevertheless, as in the teachings of the Sufi poets and some Hindu writings, Buddhists are told that although the *outer* journey can contribute significantly to the path of enlightenment, the *interior* pilgrimage can bring them closer to the goal of nirvana. Buddha told his followers, "You cannot travel the path until you have become the path."

"You cannot travel the path until you have become the path."

Buddha

Thomas Merton (who studied Buddhism and engaged in conversation with Buddhists) describes Buddhist monastic life as essentially a life of *angya*, of pilgrimage. In his book *Mystics and Zen Masters,* he writes:

> It is as a pilgrim that the newcomer presents himself at the monastery door, whether he be a monk already experienced and trained in another monastery, or a postulant newly arrived from secular life with a letter from his spiritual father. He comes on foot as a "homeless one," a wanderer, wearing the traditional

> bamboo hat and straw sandals, carrying all his belongings in a small papier-mâché box slung round his neck. . . . On his way to his chosen monastery, the pilgrim will spend the nights sleeping in temples or in roadside shrines, if not in the open fields.

The Buddhist monk's formation in a monastery teaches him that his whole life is a pilgrimage, "a search, in exile, for his true home." The "Song of Pilgrimage," composed by a Chinese Zen monk, describes, according to Merton, how a pilgrim monk is to live:

> His conduct is to be transparent as ice or crystal
>
> He is not to seek fame or wealth
>
> He is to rid himself of defilements of all sorts.
>
> He has no other way open to him but to go about and inquire;
>
> Let him be trained in mind and body by walking over the mountains and fording the rivers;
>
> Let him befriend wise men in the Dharma [Law] and pay them respect wherever he may accost them;
>
> Let him brave the snow, tread on the frosty roads, not minding the severity of the weather;
>
> Let him cross the waves and penetrate the clouds, chasing away dragons and evil spirits.

In the Sanskrit poem, "Ashokavadana," we find stories of the earliest Buddhist pilgrim, the emperor Ashoka, who from about 274–232 B.C.E. united almost all of India under his rule. His contribution to the spread of Buddhist pilgrimage was considerable. As a convert to Buddhism, he visited thirty-two Buddhist shrines in his lifetime, setting an example to all his people. A second major contribution was having relics of Buddha and his disciples collected and redistributed. He also financially supported the construction of roads, rest houses, and watering stations for pilgrims. A sure sign of his integrity was his humility in not calling any attention to his accomplishments. He stated, "These are trifling comforts. For the people have received various facilities from previous kings as well as from me. But I have done what I have primarily in order that the people may follow the path of Dharma with faith and devotion."

In about 400 C.E. another famous pilgrim made his way to the Buddhist shrines of India. A monk from China by the name of Fa-hsien wrote of his extensive travels with other Buddhist monks, which lasted fourteen years. His pilgrimage was filled, as many are, with both exhilaration and despondency. On reaching the Jetavan Grove at Shravasti where the Buddha delivered many of his most famous teachings, Fa-hsien writes (in the third person):

> When Fa-hsien and To-Ching [his companion] arrived at this temple . . . , they reflected that this was the spot where the Lord of men had passed twenty-five years of his life; they themselves, at the risk of their lives, were

> now dwelling amongst foreigners; of those who had with like purpose traveled through a succession of countries with them, some had returned home, some were now dead; and now, gazing on the place where the Buddha once dwelt but was no longer to be seen, their hearts were affected with very lively regret.

At another site located at the Vulture Peak, his emotional response is much different:

> Fa-hsien, ascending the Gridhrakuta mountain, offered his flowers and incense and lit his lamps for the night. Being deeply moved he could scarcely restrain his tears as he said, "Here it was in bygone days Buddha dwelt. . . . Fa-hsien, not privileged to be born when the Buddha lived, can but gaze on the traces of his presence and the place which he occupied."

Other pilgrims followed Fa-hsien not only to sites linked with the Buddha, but to holy places linked with those who had achieved their own form of Buddhahood. These were called bodhisattvas, the deities, saints, and masters of Buddhism, whose sacred places, relics, and stories became important to the faithful beyond India, in China, Japan, and elsewhere. In Japan, for example, places established by or associated with Japanese pilgrim-monks quickly became holy, as did aspects of their own landscape, such as the sacred mountain of Fuji, where monasteries were established.

Besides Fa-hsien, perhaps the most influential of all the Chinese pilgrims to visit India was Hsuan-tsang who was there from 629 to 645 C.E. He wrote an extensive account of his travels that appeared in twelve books, the *Si-Yu-Ki* or "Records of the Western World," a treasure-trove of information about India in the seventh century. What his account and that of the earlier Fa-hsien show is how much they were changed into Buddhas themselves, Enlightened Ones, as they followed the Buddha's way. They revealed to their readers how pilgrimage can lead to inner transformation. This is one of the major lessons of the ancient stories and great spiritual traditions, and what their proponents—and critics—say is the true meaning of pilgrimage.

"All these Cornish shores are holy,
Here the Saints in prayer did dwell,
Raising font and altar lowly
Preaching far with staff and bell—
Piran, Petroc, Paul Aurelian,
Euny, Samson, Winwaloe."

Canon G. Miles Brown, "Hymn of the Cornish Saints"

exploring a great spiritual practice

chapterthree

From Desert Pilgrims and Celtic Voyagers to Russian Saints

"In visiting the **holy places** so great was the passion and the enthusiasm she [Paula] exhibited for each, that she could never have **torn herself away** from one had she not been eager to **visit** the **rest.**"

St. Jerome, fourth century

"Do not be afraid. You will suffer **no evil.** Help for the **journey** is upon us."

The Voyage of Saint Brendan, tenth century

"All of us are **pilgrims** on this earth; I have even heard people say that the **earth** itself is a **pilgrim** in the **heavens.**"

Maxim Gorky, twentieth century

Christianity, of course, originated with Jesus, a Jewish man rooted in a spiritual tradition that honored pilgrimage. The Gospel of Luke notes that when Jesus was young, "every year his parents used to go to Jerusalem for the Feast of the Passover" (2:41). Jesus continued this custom; he celebrated his last Passover meal there (cf. Lk 22:14–20). But perhaps the *first* pilgrims in Christian history were the Magi who traveled in search of the Christ child:

> After Jesus had been born at Bethlehem in Judea during the reign of King Herod, some wise men came to Jerusalem from the east. "Where is the infant king of the Jews?" they asked. "We saw his star as it rose and have come to do him homage" (cf. Mt 2:1–12).

Filled with delight at the sight of this star, they went into the stable over which it shone, fell to their knees, and offered him gifts of gold, frankincense, and myrrh.

Jesus himself in the gospel accounts is portrayed as *the* Pilgrim *par excellance*. The very structure of the gospels is influenced by the idea of pilgrimage. The infancy narratives express this when in chapter two of Luke, for example, we find him constantly traveling with Mary and Joseph between Bethlehem and Jerusalem in Judea and Nazareth in Galilee. The gospels of Matthew, Mark, and Luke see Jesus' public ministry as unfolding in two stages. First, as an itinerant

> **"Foxes have holes and the birds of the air have nests, but the Son of Man has nowhere to lay his head."**
>
> *Matthew 9:58*

preacher, Jesus visits the villages and travels the rural areas of Galilee, and second, he makes his way to Jerusalem where he is to die. Luke even begins his "Journey to Jerusalem" narrative with Jesus' describing himself in terms that any pilgrim would understand: "Foxes have holes and the birds of the air have nests, but the Son of Man has nowhere to lay his head" (9:58). After his resurrection, he tells his disciples to take up the pilgrim's staff when he says, "Go out to the whole world; proclaim the Good News to all creation" (Mk 16:15–16). John's gospel sees Jesus as a pilgrim because he is not of this world; his life is a journey *from* God his father *to* God: Jesus says, "I came from the Father and have come into the world, and now I leave the world to go to the Father" (Jn 16:28).

Desert Pilgrims and the Holy Land

Followers of Jesus were naturally drawn to the sites and landscape where he had lived and ministered. Origen, writing in the middle of the third century, says, "There is shown at Bethlehem the cave where He [Jesus] was born . . . and this site is greatly talked of in surrounding places." Eusebius of Caesarea, the early Christian historian of the fourth century, writes regarding Jerusalem: "Believers in Christ all congregate from all parts of the world . . . that they may worship at the Mount of Olives opposite to the city." Although Christians had been persecuted for their beliefs, it was Constantine's mother, the empress Helena, who made it possible for pilgrims to journey to these holy places. When her son became the first of the Roman emperors to acknowledge Christianity, Helena visited Palestine in 326–327 C.E. She searched for relics of Jesus and the actual holy sites linked with him. Eusebius states in his *Life of Constantine*: "Though advanced in years [Helena was in her late seventies], yet gifted with no common degree of wisdom, she hastened with youthful speed to survey this venerable land." Through her efforts churches in Bethlehem and on the Mount of Olives were built.

Many pilgrims followed Helena's example, especially after the True Cross on which Jesus died was found. Constantine began to build other Christian churches in Jerusalem, including the Church of the Holy Sepulcher, where the Emperor Hadrian, according to St. Jerome, had earlier built a temple to Venus. Latins came from Rome and Western Europe as pilgrims, as well as Greeks from Constantinople and Eastern Europe, Armenians from Asia Minor, and others from Syria and

Ethiopia. Some pilgrims decided to stay and settle near the holy sites in what came to be called "the Holy Land." Many early pilgrims came at great personal expense and all traveled at considerable risk, for, as one of them said, "We suffered much on our journey and came very near to losing our lives."

Some came with less than noble motivations. One story tells how Mary, a fifth century prostitute from Alexandria, decided to visit Jerusalem:

While I was living in this way, one summer I saw a great crowd of men, Egyptians and Libyans, going down toward the sea. I stopped one of them and asked him where they were going in such haste. He told me, "They are all going to Jerusalem for the Exaltation of the Holy Cross which is to be celebrated there in a few days time."

Mary decided to join them. She paid for her passage onboard a ship with her body, as it were, seducing whomever she could, and upon arriving in Jerusalem, continued to sell herself, according to a biography, to "both the citizens and those who were there as pilgrims." Only when she was prevented from entering the church by some invisible force did she repent. She became one of the great desert mothers, known as St. Mary of Egypt.

Only when she was prevented from entering the church by some invisible force did she repent. She became one of the great **desert mothers,** known as **Saint Mary of Egypt.**

Pilgrims continued to come to the desert regions. They were attracted by the holy sites, and they sought guidance from the holy men and women who were building hermitages and monasteries there. In the fourth century, one monastic founder, Basil the Great, journeyed from Cappadocia to visit the desert with his brother Gregory of Nyssa and their sister Macrina. Gregory later wrote a letter condemning the practice of pilgrimage, pointing out that "when the Lord invites the blest to their inheritance in the kingdom of Heaven, He does not include a pilgrimage to Jerusalem among their good deeds." Gregory's primary argument was that what ultimately mattered in spiritual terms was the heart of every person—not the places he or she had visited on pilgrimage.

Augustine, among others, agreed with Gregory. The famous bishop of Hippo stated that "God is everywhere, it is true, and

"God is everywhere, it is true, and He that made all things is not contained or confined to dwell in any place."

St. Augustine

He that made all things is not contained or confined to dwell in any place." Augustine wrote in *The City of God* that our time on earth is a pilgrimage to God: "For, the true City of the saints is in heaven, though here on earth it produces citizens in whom it wanders as on a pilgrimage through time looking for the Kingdom of eternity" (Book 15, ch. 1).

About 380 C.E., two young friends, John Cassian and Germanus, set out to visit the holy places of Palestine. In Bethlehem, they joined a monastery near the cave of the Nativity and remained there for several years. After what the younger man called "too short a training," they moved on to Egypt, where for the next fifteen years or so they lived with various desert hermits. Cassian described his experiences in two books, *Institutes* and *Conferences,* which highly influenced the establishment of monasticism in the East and the West.

In 385, St. Jerome traveled to Egypt with a wealthy Roman woman named Paula, and her daughter, Eustochium; from there the three went on together to Palestine. Jerome describes Paula's eagerness as a pilgrim when she visited the holy sites:

> Moreover, in visiting the holy places so great was the passion and the enthusiasm she exhibited for each, that she could never have torn herself away from one had she not been eager to visit the rest. Before the Cross she threw herself down in adoration as though she beheld the Lord hanging upon it; and when she entered the tomb which was the scene of the Resurrection she kissed the stone which the angel had rolled away from the door of the sepulcher.

In 386 the three pilgrim-companions settled down in Bethlehem in a spacious cave where Jerome did his translating and writing—with the support and scholarly help of the two women. Like Gregory of Nyssa, Jerome had his own reservations about pilgrimage. He warned one prospective pilgrim, Paulinus of Nola, that he could expect to see Jerusalem as "a crowded city with the whole variety of people you find in such centers, prostitutes, actors, and clowns." On the whole, however, Jerome approved of pilgrimage to the Holy Land, and his letters on the subject persuaded many others to follow in his, Paula's, and Eustochium's footsteps.

One who did in the early fifth century was Egeria, the nun from Galicia in Spain that we encountered earlier. She visited Mount Sinai and other sacred sites, including the churches in Jerusalem, where she participated in the Holy Week liturgies. She mentions how, at one liturgy on Good Friday, a number of deacons had to stand near the bishop to guard the wood of the True Cross, because someone had tried to bite off a piece! Relics of Jesus and the saints were obviously gaining in importance.

We know too of Celtic pilgrims who visited the desert lands. The Irish, in particular, were known for their frequent travels. As Gozbert, author of a *Life of St. Gall*, remarked, "Of late so many Irish are pilgrims that it would appear that the habit of travel is second-nature to them." These pilgrims came to pray at the holy sites, hoping to gain insights that would enrich their lives and deepen their spirituality.

The Irish and St. Brendan's Story

The Irish church blossomed within a century after the death of St. Patrick in 462. Great monasteries, influenced by John Cassian's writings and the family-oriented pagan Celtic culture, arose at Clonard, Clonmacnoise, Kildare, Armagh, Derry, Durrow, and Bangor. The monastery at Bangor produced hundreds of missionary-pilgrims who spread the Christian faith throughout the continent of Europe. Spiritual leaders, such as St. Columbanus and St. Gall set sail for the mainland. They built monasteries at Luxeuil in France, St. Gallen in Switzerland, and Bobbio in Italy. Along with these better-known saints, vast numbers of Irish monks poured into France and then traveled on to Belgium, Switzerland, Austria, southern Germany, and northern Italy. Some went even further, into modern Poland, Hungary, and Russia. From the seventh century until the middle of the eighth century, these Irish monks, joined by Anglo-Saxon missionaries, became the most important religious and cultural influence affecting the Carolingian empire and eventually all of medieval Europe. Their travel, *peregrinatio*, as it was called, was the practice of wandering for the love of God—sometimes with, sometimes without, a fixed destination.

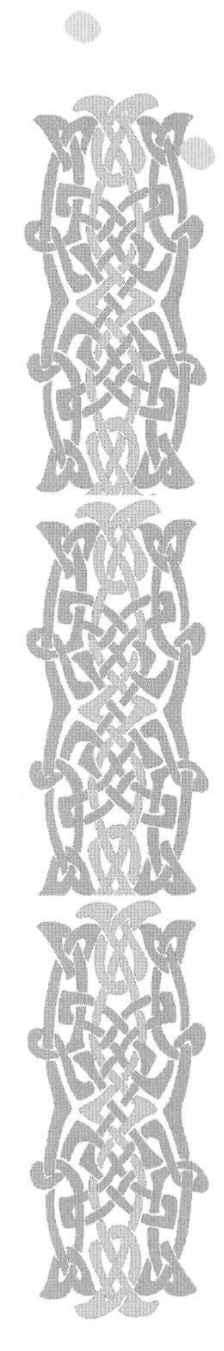

These early pilgrims, missionaries, and voyagers shared a desire to travel, to visit foreign shores, to bring the message of the gospel to those who had not heard it. In contrast to the "red martyrdom" of giving one's life up for Christ or the "green martyrdom" of participating in severe penitential practices, they were willing to face the long, hard "white martyrdom" of living years far from home and the warmth of one's hearth. Despite the pain of that separation, the historian John T. McNeill tells us in *The Celtic Churches* (University of Chicago Press, 1974), "For more than half a millennium a stream of educated and dedicated men poured from the monasteries of Ireland to 'go on pilgrimage for Christ' wherever they might feel themselves divinely led."

The *Anglo-Saxon Chronicle* tells of pilgrim-monks who wandered *without* a fixed destination. One day in 891, three Irishmen landed on the coast of Cornwall in a boat that had no oars. The three of them had said that they wanted "to live in a state of pilgrimage, for the love of God, they cared not where," so they left Ireland and took enough food for seven days. They reached Cornwall just in time. They, of course, were the lucky ones—we don't know what happened to the countless others who possibly never reached a nearby shore! Clearly, the story reveals that this practice was not all that uncommon, and that a primary aspect of it was trust in God.

Another Celtic story, *The Voyage of Saint Brendan*, became one of the most famous and enduring stories of western Christianity. Based upon earlier Irish literary and oral traditions about the saint who lived in the sixth century, and probably based on the stories of the *Odyssey* and the *Aeneid* as well, this story reflects an Irish monk's search for the Promised Land. According to Carl Jung, heroes are usually portrayed as wanderers, and their wandering is a symbol of their longing for transformation, holiness, union with God. St. Brendan was such a hero from Clonfert in western Ireland. In the opening of his story, he is visited by a monk called Barrind who tells him a fascinating tale about his own journey to a mysterious island in the west called the Promised Land. Brendan is intrigued, calls his fellow-monks together, and asks their opinion on what to do. "From you who are dear to me," he says, "and share the good fights with me I look for advice and help, for my heart and all my thoughts are fixed on one determination . . . to go in search of the Promised Land of the Saints." He demonstrates a spirit of collaboration (a necessary quality for any pilgrim) when he asks them, "How does this seem to you? What advice would you give?"

Their response is positive. Together they build a boat of wood, covered with ox-hides and smeared with oil; together they embark, steering westwards; together they "have decided to be pilgrims for the days of our life that remain." For the next seven years they traverse the seas, making progress, but sailing in a circular pattern, as they visit the same islands and monastic sites on the same liturgical feasts. They encounter a friendly whale named Jasconius where they celebrate the vigil of Easter each year, and an island called "the Paradise of Birds," with groves of trees and flowers everywhere. On their first visit, a beautiful white bird prophesies to Brendan that he will find, eventually, "what you cherish in your heart, that is, the Promised Land of the Saints." They meet other human guides who direct them to the next place and encourage them to keep going, despite their weariness. On another island, they meet the monastic Community of Ailbe. They are hospitably welcomed, as pilgrims were in the Middle Ages, with the kiss of peace and the washing of their feet (clearly a wonderful custom for foot-sore pilgrims). Here they celebrate Christmas each year. They also visit an island of gigantic grapes, a crystal pillar in the sea, an island of metalsmiths, and an island where a hermit named Paul lives. They even meet Judas, the betrayer of Christ, stranded alone on a rock out on the ocean. (He is actually quite happy there, since, because of Christ's compassion, he is given a reprieve from the fires of hell on Sundays and certain feasts!)

They repeat this cycle for six years, until finally in the seventh year they reach the Promised Land. A youth meets them, and explains why it took them so long: "You could not find it immediately because God wanted to show you his varied secrets in the great ocean." They explore the island for forty days, enjoying its beauty, until they are instructed to return home where all are welcomed back. Brendan thanks his community for their love, and proceeds to tell the story of what happened on the journey, "and the great and marvellous wonders God had deigned to show him." Shortly after, he dies, a pilgrim traveling to be with God and the saints in heaven, the true Promised Land.

Scholars debate whether Brendan actually made the voyage. He was known as a voyager who traveled at least around the British Isles and possibly to Brittany in France. Some believe the stories describe real places, and that Brendan did reach Greenland and Newfoundland. Whether historically true or not, his story was translated from Latin into numerous languages, including French, Breton, Flemish, and Welsh. It inspired many to set sail as pilgrims and explorers, including Christopher Columbus, who read the work.

Brendan's story also is a paradigm of pilgrimage, in which one sets out with a definite goal, meets difficulties, and finally reaches one's destination. It began with his decision, endorsed by others, to follow his heart. Brendan offered his colleagues encouragement with words that any pilgrim might find helpful: "Do not be afraid. You will suffer no evil. Help for the journey is upon us." And words which the Irish monks who landed on the shores of Cornwall would appreciate: "Is not the all-powerful God the pilot and sailor of our boat? Leave it to him. He himself guides our journey as he wills."

"Is not the all-powerful God the pilot and sailor of our boat? Leave it to him. He himself guides our journey as he wills."

St. Brendan

Becoming pilgrims or wanderers for Christ, of course, was not limited to the Irish. Pilgrimage emerged in the Middle Ages as one of the most prevalent expressions of religious devotion throughout the Christian world. It seems everyone who could go did go on pilgrimage, from kings and bishops to monks and millers. The emperor Charlemagne traveled to Rome at least four times in the late eighth century.

Although male pilgrims seem to have predominated (probably due to safety concerns for women, their family responsibilities, and the lack of money to travel), there were notable exceptions. An English laywoman in the fourteenth century, Margery Kempe, who had fourteen children and briefly ran the largest brewery in Lynn, traveled on numerous pilgrimages in and outside of her country. Felix Fabri, a Dominican friar from Ulm, Germany, also tells of certain wealthy elderly women who traveled with him to the Holy Land in the 1480s. While certain knights were displeased by their presence, the friar welcomed them into his group and noted how, on the return home when almost everyone fell sick on board the ship, it was the "ancient matrons" who graciously acted as nurses.

Roads and ships throughout Europe were crowded with thousands of pilgrims trying to reach the three great centers of Christian pilgrimage: Rome with its catacombs, fine churches, and the relics of Sts. Peter and Paul; the East, especially

Palestine, Egypt, Syria, St. Catherine's Monastery in the Sinai, and the great city of Constantinople; and, by the ninth century, Santiago de Compostela in Spain, where the relics of St. James had been discovered and were honored. ("Compostela" means "field of the star," a designation based on the story that a heavenly light had shown on the place of James' tomb.)

Other popular sites in England included Canterbury, Walsingham, Glastonbury, and the Saints' Way, a route through Cornwall followed by pilgrims on foot, from the harbor town of Padstow in the north to the southern port of Fowey. In Ireland, Croagh Patrick, Lough Derg, Glendalough, and the Aran Islands were the four major sites; in Wales, Bardsey Island and St. David's. The peripatetic twelfth-century churchman Gerald of Wales describes both Ireland and Wales in his fascinating writings on his travels there, including a description of the monastery of St. Brigid at Kildare which kept a fire always lit and possessed an illuminated gospel book whose artistry, he said, was "the work, not of men, but of angels." Along with the archangel St. Raphael, this same Brigid was considered the patron saint of pilgrims during the Middle Ages.

The monastery of St. Brigid at Kildare which kept a fire always lit and possessed an illuminated gospel book whose artistry was "the work, not of men, but of angels."

In France pilgrims traveled to Tours where St. Martin was buried, Poitiers to see the relics of St. Hilary (mentor of St. Martin and writer on the Holy Trinity), Chartres, which had a garment worn by Mary, Vezelay, which was said to have the relics of Mary Magdalene, Conques with its famous golden image of St. Foy, and Mont St. Michel, dedicated (as so many high places were) to St. Michael the Archangel. One of the major pilgrim routes to Santiago, which was visited by more than half a million pilgrims each year in the eleventh and twelfth centuries, began in Paris at a church named for St. James. (Unfortunately, only a tower, Tour St.-Jacques, remains today at the site, since the church was razed to the ground during the French Revolution.) This pilgrim route proceeded through the heart of Paris on Rue St.-Jacques, a major road since Roman times, and on down through Tours, Poitiers, Bordeaux, and across northern Spain to Santiago de Compostela.

People went on pilgrimage to major and minor sites for a variety of reasons: as a penance for one's sins, as an expression of gratitude for divine grace, as an opportunity for widening one's knowledge or deepening one's faith. Others went to find solace or healing. Some people perhaps simply wanted to get away, escape responsibilities and see something new! Others set forth, concerned for their soul, their salvation, and used the pilgrimage as a form of soul-making, preparing for a "happy death." This motivation was certainly reinforced by the religious art they encountered. From Celtic high crosses depicting the Last Judgment to stained-glass windows and the carvings over cathedral doors, showing the same scene, medieval pilgrims were encouraged to be aware of the consequences of their life choices, and take the better path.

Others set forth, concerned for their soul, their salvation, and used the pilgrimage as a form of soul-making, preparing for a "happy death."

Sometimes pilgrimage was undertaken for the purpose of obtaining liturgical books and art for specific monasteries and libraries. Bede the Venerable in eighth-century England, for example, describes how Benedict Biscop, the founder of his Benedictine monastery in Jarrow, made five pilgrimages to Rome for that purpose. Biscop also brought back, Bede says,

"an abundant supply of relics of the apostles and Christian martyrs." Relics had become increasingly in demand since the second Nicene Council (787 C.E.) had decreed that every church and altar was to have at least one.

This respect for relics goes back to the earliest days of the church when special veneration was given to the mortal remains of martyrs. When the martyr Polycarp was killed in Smyrna in 155, his fellow Christians recorded, "We recovered his bones, rarer than gold and more precious than costly jewels. We laid them in a fitting place." If the saints in heaven were not only models of behavior but also soul friends of the living, then to have their physical remains or something they had owned or touched would give individual Christians and their communities special favor. As in the royal courts of medieval society, saints could act as petitioners and emissaries for ordinary Christians at the court of God. They could bestow benefits, heal the sick, grant miracles.

The shadow side of such veneration was the theft of relics (sometimes one church or monastery would steal from the other) and the indiscriminate sale of forgeries, especially after the Crusaders intermittently conquered the Holy Land and brought back all sorts of bizarre fakes. The sack of Constantinople in 1204 put a whole new wave of "relics" on the market, including Jesus' crown of thorns. King Louis IX of France built the exquisite Sainte-Chapelle in Paris to house this valuable relic, paying more money for it than it took to build the entire church, which was designed to look like a giant reliquary.

Surely there were and are true relics, worthy of respect and veneration, but one wonders at the gullibility of medieval Christians when they were told that certain pilgrim sites had vials of Mary's milk, or sweat from St. Martin of Tours, or the finger of St. Thomas the Apostle that had touched the risen Christ—not to mention Jesus' foreskin, umbilical cord, and hairs from his beard! Among Canterbury's relics was clay supposedly from which Adam had been created!

When churchmen discovered that pilgrimage was a profit-making enterprise, some were unscrupulous in their deeds. At Boxley in England, a life-size figure of Christ was so rigged that it rolled its eyes, shed tears, and foamed at the mouth for pilgrims, while at another site in Kent, the Christ-figure nodded its head, winked its eyes, and bowed at the waist to receive the prayers (and money) of the devout. Sometimes, it seems, more than one church had the same relics. A story concerning one pilgrim traveling to various shrines tells how, when he was shown the skull of John the Baptist at a certain monastery, he remarked that the skull of the same saint had been exhibited to him only the day before at another abbey. "Maybe," the custodian-monk replied, "that was the skull of John the Baptist when a young man, whereas this in our possession is his skull after he was fully advanced in years and wisdom."

Another despicable aspect of pilgrim trade and relics concerns the dissection of the saints' bodies, apparently sometimes it seems before they were even cold. Within hours of her death, St. Catherine was

Another despicable aspect of pilgrim trade and relics concerns the dissection of the saints' bodies, apparently sometimes it seems before they were even cold.

decapitated. Her head was put on display in a church in Siena (where it can still be seen today), while her body resides in Rome. In Spain, at Alba de Tormes, the heart and forearm of the sixteenth-century mystic, St. Teresa, are on display in separate reliquaries, and her ring-finger (with the ring still on it!) is at the Monastery of the Incarnation in Avila. For many sincere contemporary pilgrims, body parts are not a source of inspiration but of revulsion. Considering this dark side of medieval spirituality, it is understandable why there was such a reaction among sincere Christians at the time of the Protestant Reformation.

Still, pilgrims flocked to the shrines of the saints, encouraged by the privileges which were soon promoted legally. If one was a priest, for example, it was legislated that he could draw his full salary as long as he wasn't absent for more than three years; if a layman, he was excused the payment of all taxes while he was gone. Laws also protected him from being arrested or cast into prison, while his property at home was secure from confiscation. If a person was not able, for whatever reason, to travel, someone could be hired to go in one's place. This performance of religious duties and penance by proxy was a fairly common practice in the Middle Ages.

As a result of so many people traveling on pilgrimage, a great "white mantle of churches," according to the eleventh-century monk, Radulph Glaber, was built across the European landscape to accommodate them. Monasteries and churches were constructed and, Glaber says, "consecrated to all sorts of saints, and even the little chapels in villages were reconstructed by the faithful more beautiful than before." Inns, too, were created in villages and cities for the pilgrim trade, and medieval society as a whole prospered because of it. Some of the larger monasteries, such as the Cistercian monastery of Cluny in Burgundy, France, also served pilgrims in other ways, notably by building hospices, hostels, and bridges on pilgrim roads to Santiago de Compostela. Guidebooks also were written. Aymery Picaud, a monk from near Poitiers, created the popular *Pilgrim's Guide to Santiago* around 1150, which advised pilgrims on places to travel and people to avoid.

Reaction, Reformation, and Revival

In the fifteenth century numerous church leaders cried out for people to stay home, especially monks, recommending to them the vow of stability that the Rule of St. Benedict supported. By the eve of the Protestant reformation in the sixteenth century, more people had become disillusioned. Critics of the practice, like Erasmus of Rotterdam, commented on the immorality of some pilgrims—as Gregory of Nyssa had done centuries before. Martin Luther, who had gone to Rome on pilgrimage as a young monk and been, according to some accounts, thoroughly scandalized by what he saw there, later wrote (after he had been excommunicated): "All pilgrimages should be stopped. There is no good in them." He probably would have agreed with an eighth-century Irish poem, "To go to Rome means great toil and little profit. The (heavenly) king whom you seek can only be found there if you bring him within yourself." Others followed Luther's stance, repulsed by the selling of indulgences to remove the punishment of sin after death, and what they considered to be the over-emphasis on "works," one of which was pilgrimage.

"To go to Rome means great toil and little profit. The (heavenly) king whom you seek can only be found there if you bring him within yourself."

Eighth-Century Irish poem

Yet even after the closing of monasteries and the tragic destruction of so many shrines, the idea of pilgrimage lingered on. It was expressed vividly in the spiritual classic *Pilgrim's Progress,* first published in 1678, by John Bunyan, a Puritan writer. This story revolves around a pilgrim named Christian and his struggle through trials, temptations, and tribulations to reach the Celestial City, a metaphor for heaven. Another writer, the English poet William Wordsworth, epitomizes the Romantic sensibility (and nostalgia) that flourished in the 18th century: the sense that certain landscapes, dotted with monastic ruins, are evocative of past glory, and have a numinous quality to them. As he says in "Lines Composed a Few Miles Above Tintern Abbey" (in Wales):

> Five years have passed; five summers, with the length
> Of five long winters! and again I hear
> These waters, rolling from their mountain-springs
> With a soft inland murmur.—Once again
> Do I behold these steep and lofty cliffs,
> That on a wild secluded scene impress
> Thoughts of more deep seclusion; and connect
> the landscape with the quiet of the sky. . . .
> For I have learned
> To look on nature, not as in the hour
> Of thoughtless youth; but hearing oftentimes
> The still, sad music of humanity. . . .
> And I have felt
> A presence that disturbs me with the joy
> Of elevated thoughts; a sense sublime
> Of something far more deeply interfused. . . .

By the twentieth century, Protestant distrust and antipathy toward pilgrimages began to fade as more people realized the value of connecting with their ancestors, including those spiritual leaders held in high esteem. Thousands of staunch

Lutheran pilgrims, for example, journeyed to sites associated with Luther in 1983, the five-hundredth anniversary of his birth. Meanwhile, Roman Catholics continued to emphasize the value of pilgrimage (after their own sixteenth-century Counter-Reformation), making their way to the old shrines as well as to newer ones, frequently linked with the Virgin Mary, especially those in located in France at Lourdes, in Portugal at Fatima, in Mexico at Guadalupe, and in Bosnia-Herzegovina at Medjugorje. Today Celtic enthusiasts, and Catholic, Protestant, and New-Age seekers, with a spirituality that transcends denominational differences—make their way to Iona, Scotland, and to the other prominent sites of the Celtic saints in Wales, Northumbria, Cornwall, Brittany, Galicia, and, of course, Ireland. The ecumenical community founded by Brother Roger, Taizé, draws thousands of pilgrims to France each year.

Eastern Orthodox Christians too have their own devotion to the practice. Immersed in a literature and rich history of pilgrimage, perhaps the most beautiful expression of their spirituality is found in *The Way of a Pilgrim*, written

His journey led him to a *staretz*, a Russian spiritual guide, who taught him the Jesus Prayer, and helped him, in turn, guide others.

by an anonymous Russian Christian in the nineteenth century. It tells the story of a layman in search of wisdom who traveled through Russia and Siberia. He visited monasteries and shrines of the saints, hoping to learn how to "pray without ceasing." His journey led him to a *staretz*, a Russian spiritual guide, who taught him the Jesus Prayer, and helped him, in turn, guide others. Other Russian writers, from Fyodor Dostoevsky to Maxim Gorky, have endorsed the practice of pilgrimage, with the latter perhaps stating best what so many in our day have come to realize: "All of us are pilgrims on this earth; I have even heard people say that the earth itself is a pilgrim in the heavens."

"When I feel myself discouraged in the midst of my pilgrimages, I say to myself, "If I wish for the result, I must take the means," and under this thought I persevere. I do more: scarcely am I again in my own abode, when I think of recommencing my travels. Perpetual travel would be a delightful way of passing life, especially for one who cannot conform to the ideas that govern the world in the age in which he lives. To change one's country is tantamount to changing one's century."

Astolphe de Custine, Letters from Russia

chapter four

exploring a great spiritual practice

Stages of Pilgrimage

"No one should think visiting the **holy places** to be a light task; there is the intense heat of the sun, the walking from place to place, **kneeling** and **prostration.**"

Felix Fabri

"We shall not cease from **exploration**
And the end of all our exploring
Will be to arrive where we started
And know the place for the **first time.**"

T. S. Eliot

As we look back at the history of pilgrimage, we can discern a pattern. There are different stages to this sacred travel. Knowing the pattern may give prospective pilgrims some sense of what to expect. For pilgrims who have recently returned, knowing the pattern may aid them in naming their experiences. I have found this to be true in my own pilgrim travels or when I am preparing groups to leave with me on a new spiritual adventure. I think the stages of pilgrimage resemble the stages of personal change as described by two authors in particular. We will look at each one.

French anthropologist Arnold van Gennep, in *Les Rites du Passage* (Routledge and Kegan Paul, 1960), first published in 1909, examines how people make transitions from childhood to adulthood or from non-membership (or marginal membership) to full membership in a community. Van Gennep associated this pattern of personal, social, and psychological change with ritual processes and rites. He said that this transformation consists of three stages: *separation* [separation], *marge* [transition], and *agregation* [incorporation]. He shows how all rites of passage are marked by these three phases: the detachment of the individual or group from an earlier social structure; the entrance into a liminal state or realm that has few or none of the attributes of the past or coming state; and the return to social life with new rights, obligatio responsibilities.

Joseph Campbell, a scholar of mythology, later adapted these ideas to his work with stories and myths of religious and cultural heroes. In his classic, *The Hero With a Thousand Faces* (Princeton University Press, 1973), Campbell presupposes that the great myths of a culture or religious tradition are really about an individual's spiritual and psychological maturation. He posits that, despite the infinite variety of particulars found in the heroic myths of the world, there is an underlying common pattern or "monomyth" that describes how an individual becomes a hero. Becoming a "hero" for Campbell means becoming a more mature person, psychologically, socially, and spiritually. Campbell identifies several stages in this process.

In the first stage, which Campbell calls "departure" or "the call to adventure," the hero leaves home or that which is familiar to him or her—whether it's a certain routine, job, or way of living. The invitation to leave can come at any time, and can be expressed in all sorts of subtle and sometimes dramatic ways. If the person accepts

Campbell assures us that at this stage, as it is reflected in the mythic stories, help is often given unexpectedly through human, angelic, or even animal mentors.

this invitation, he or she is propelled into the next stage. Campbell calls it the stage of "initiation" or "the road of trials." The person enters a painful liminal or marginal state filled with ambiguity and usually great anxiety. One has left the familiar but has as yet not reached another stage. This liminality or marginality is frequently experienced as a very lonely journey in which certain tasks must be accomplished and temptations met. Though these may seem overwhelming, Campbell assures us that at this stage, as it is reflected in the mythic stories, help is often given unexpectedly through human, angelic, or even animal mentors. They enter the hero's life when they are most needed, and they guide the person through this second stage. Benefiting from such help, a person survives this passage and finds "the treasure," receives a "blessing," becomes "master of two worlds." He or she gains wisdom and enters the last stage.

The "return" is when a person who has not merely survived the road of trials but prospered from it returns to his or her homeland, tribe, or community and shares what he or she has learned. This return, of course, may result in another new adventure or wilderness sojourn. Campbell says there is a new experience of personal freedom, centeredness, and clarity of vision in this last stage. The hero feels a new level of integration with his or her deeper self and God.

Drawing upon the work of these two scholars, we now consider how the stages of pilgrimage relate to these stages of personal change.

Call to Adventure

The call to set forth on pilgrimage can occur in numerous ways. Sometimes the invitation comes through a specific event that sets us to thinking about the possibility of travel. In John Bunyan's allegorical *Pilgrim's Progress* the call comes through a dream:

> As I walked through the wilderness of this world, I lighted on a certain place, where was a den; and I laid me down in that place to sleep; and as I slept I dreamed a dream. I dreamed, and behold I saw a man clothed with rags, standing in a certain place, with his face from his own house, a book in his hand, and a great burden upon his back. I looked, and saw him open the book, and read therein; and as he read, he wept and trembled; and not being able longer to contain, he brake out with a lamentable cry; saying, "What shall I do?"

This cry of the heart that precedes setting out on a meaningful journey is ultimately the recognition of dissatisfaction in one's life. Underlying this dissatisfaction is the desire for change. In Bunyan's story, such desire is what set the main character, Christian, on a pilgrimage through the Slough of Despond, Vanity Fair, and the Hill of Difficulty on to the Celestial City. Christian wanted something more than his present life was offering. He wanted some relief from the burden on his back; he wanted some direction, some guidance on what to do next. Pilgrimage is often a search for answers to serious questions in a person's life. It may be a quest for healing or spiritual guidance.

Pilgrimage is often a search for answers to serious questions in a person's life. It may be a quest for healing or spiritual guidance.

At other times the call to pilgrimage might come through someone's invitation. The person may be an acquaintance, a lifelong friend, or even a total stranger. As we saw in the story of St. Brendan, his desire to search for the Promised Land originated with a certain monk, St. Barrind, whom Brendan didn't seem to know that well, but who told him about the mysterious island in the west. Because of Barrind's tale, Brendan decided to set sail to a place he hadn't even heard of before. Many of humankind's myths and stories begin with a "call to adventure" that has its origins with some mysterious person who invites the hero to reimagine his or her life.

Jim Forest, a respected peace activist, describes in his book *Pilgrim to the Russian Church* how his friendship with Dorothy Day influenced his fascination with Russian spirituality and his eventual desire to visit Russia:

> A few years later, having found my way to religious belief, I joined the Catholic Worker community in New York City. While there, I came to know the community's founder, Dorothy Day, and the special devotion she had to Russian writers, Dostoevsky most of all, but many others, including Gorky, Tolstoy, Chekhov, and Solzhenitsyn. This was matched by her love of the Russian Orthodox Church. Several times she took me with her to attend the Orthodox liturgy sung in Slavonic.

Day also introduces him to others who were interested in Russian Orthodox Spirituality. The entire experience led Forest to his becoming a pilgrim himself to Russia and eventually a convert to Russian Orthodoxy. Dorothy Day was his friend, initiator, mentor, and guide.

My own travel to Hawaii for the first time in 2002 with my family happened because John, a former student and friend, asked me to house-sit for him on Maui while he was away at Christmas. I had never been that fascinated with Hawaii; I associated it primarily with commercialism and tourism. Even when he suggested I might find its history and culture helpful for my future research and writing, I demurred. "No," I told him, "going to Hawaii is probably not a possibility, but thank you anyway." John persisted, telling me about the beauty of the landscape, and suggesting I at least bring the invitation to JoAnne. I was still not convinced, but precisely because of his persistence, I asked JoAnne if she would consider going. "Yes," she responded immediately, "if we can bring the boys." What followed during those two weeks at Christmas through New Year's was a journey that started primarily as a vacation for us but for me turned into a spiritual awakening. And all because of a friend's unexpected invitation and persistence. Pilgrimage can be like that.

Sometimes leaving home and becoming a pilgrim happens because of a kinship with ancestors, familial or spiritual, whom one wants to get to know more intimately. This desire for connection often begins at midlife when people who are increasingly aware of their mortality want to know more about their lineage and their faith. Carl Jung speaks of the "collective unconscious" or "ancestral memories" in his writings. He says that to regain our souls we need to pay attention to our ancestors, who often have much to teach us about our own vocation and identity, especially when we reach the second half of life. Still, a person does not have to be old to want to connect with ancestors or heroes of the faith. Ibn Battua, a fourteenth-century Muslim pilgrim, describes his journey to Mecca:

> I left Tangier, my birthplace, the 13th of June, 1325, being at the time twenty-two years of age, with the intention of making the Pilgrimage to the Holy House [at Mecca] and the Tomb of the Prophet [at Medina]. I set out alone, finding no companions to cheer the way with friendly intercourse, and no party of travelers with whom to associate myself. Swayed by an overwhelming impulse within me, and a long-cherished desire to visit all those glorious sanctuaries, I resolved to leave all my friends both female and male, to abandon my home as birds abandon the nest.

Carl Jung says that to regain our souls we need to pay attention to our ancestors, who often have much to teach us about our own vocation and identity, especially when we reach the second half of life.

At times the cherished memories of a beloved site or beautiful landscape can invite us to return. When I returned to the long, bleak Minnesota winter after my Hawaii trip, I found many old-time Hawaiian songs that express this "call." "Waikiki" by Andy Cummings, says quite explicitly, "Waikiki at night when the shadows are falling, I hear your surf calling . . . to me . . . ; my thoughts are always returning to you across the sea . . . the magic of Waikiki." Or in "Across the Sea," by Ernest Ka'ai, Ray Kinney, and Johnny Noble, we find other allusions: "Across the sea an isle is calling me, calling to the wanderer to return, bidding me to come back to fair Hawaii, to the sunny isles across the sea." In another song with its haunting lyrics and explicit title, "Hawaii Calls," by Harry Owens, there are the words: "Hawaii calls with a melody of love dear, across the sea as evening falls."

Memories of beauty and beautiful places have their own allure, as Edwin Mullins learned at the monastery of Santo Domingo de Silos on his way to Santiago de Compostela (see chapter one). We naturally search as pilgrims for a beauty that speaks of eternity.

In *My Quest for Beauty,* Rollo May describes his pilgrimage to Mount Athos in 1932 as a young man. This Holy Mountain, the center of Greek Orthodox monastic life, is located off the coast of Greece. May spent a week there and wrote reflections on that time.

> As we steamed out of the harbor I leaned on the railing, looking back at the cerulean sea comforting the shore of Mt. Athos. I knew I would never forget the old monk who looked like Leonardo da Vinci, or Friar Tuck, or the cook who was so proud of his halvah. That noon as I stood by the ship's rail I was thinking especially of the Easter service at the monastery of Stavronikita. . . . At the conclusion of the service we filed in front of the abbot, who, while giving each of us three Easter eggs wrapped in a veil, greeted us with the words, "*Christos Anesti*!"—which means "Christ has risen." To which each of us responded, according to the custom, "*Alethos Anesti*!"—"Truly He has risen." I remember that I had been seized then by a moment of spiritual reality: what would it mean for our world if He had truly risen?"

He then asks the question, "But what was the particular spiritual quality of this place, what was its genie?" He answers, "It came from the beauty of the mountain and the foothills, which seemed as though nature had portioned out her secrets guardedly elsewhere but here had lavished every kind of beauty from its treasure chest."

Mount Athos was for him a combination of physical and spiritual beauty that spoke to him of the eternal, of God.

Road of Trials, Marginal Places

While pilgrimages may result in encounters with the sacred, they can also be painful journeys into the unknown. We may be far from family and friends and all those things that give us a sense of self-worth and identity. This is an experience of being in the wilderness, of being betwixt and between. Pilgrims may be filled with excitement and hope. But they also may be filled with anxiety; they may worry about safety or their ability to adapt to a strange environment. Pilgrims cross a threshold and enter a new dimension, a liminal, perhaps dangerous, place.

Ancient and medieval peoples recognized this and did not take up pilgrimage lightly. They knew from a multitude of stories relayed back to them about pilgrims who had had difficult journeys or who had died along the way. In the *Life of St. Kevin of Glendalough* in Ireland, we find this story:

> One day when two women were coming on a pilgrimage to Kevin's church, robbers met them at the pass, stripped them, and beheaded them. When the news came to Kevin, he went quickly to see the

women, and put their heads on their trunks, so that they were restored to life by him.

Thank God for Kevin's timely action, but, of course, not all murdered pilgrims were so lucky as to have their heads restored!

Pilgrims cross a threshold and enter a new dimension, a liminal, perhaps dangerous, place.

The fifteenth-century Dominican friar Felix Fabri has left his own account of his two trips to the Holy Land, *Evagatorium in Terrae Sanctae* [*Wandering in the Holy Land*]. As he makes clear, even after arriving safely at one's destination, a pilgrim's difficulties may persist:

> No one should think visiting the holy places to be a light task; there is the intense heat of the sun, the walking from place to place, kneeling and prostration; above all there is the strain which everyone puts on himself striving with all his might to rouse himself in earnest piety and comprehension of what is shown him in the holy places, and to devout prayer and meditation, all which cannot be done without great fatigue, because to do them fitly a man should be at rest and not walking about. To struggle after mental

abstraction while bodily walking from place to place is exceedingly toilsome.

Despite this fatigue, Brother Fabri continued to have a consuming desire to return to the Holy Land because of the joy that he associated with it.

Medieval western pilgrims in particular were aware that to take up the pilgrim's staff amounted to answering a special call. To set forth on pilgrimage was more than an individual decision; it called for communal discernment, encouragement, endorsement, blessings. Before a pilgrim departed, the staff and satchel (called a "scrip" in which documents, money, and food were kept) were blessed by a priest in a church ceremony, so that they would be given spiritual protection. This ritual was described in the *Sarum Missal* of 1554. A pilgrim first confessed his or her sins, then lay on the floor before the altar as the priest and choir sang suitable psalms, such as the twenty-fourth:

To Yahweh belong earth and all it holds,
the world and all who lie in it;
he himself founded it on the ocean,

based it firmly on the nether sea.
Who has the right to climb the mountain of Yahweh,
who has the right to stand in his holy place?
He whose hands are clean, whose heart is pure,
whose soul does not pay homage to worthless things
and who never swears to lie.

The priest then blessed the articles, invoking the protection of Christ, and sprinkled holy water on them; he anointed the staff and handed it over with the words, "Take this staff as a support during your journey and the toils of your pilgrimage, that you may be victorious against the bands of the enemy and safely arrive at the shrine of the saints to which you wish to go and, your journey accomplished, may return to us in good health."

Communal support was a tremendous help for any pilgrim. Those left behind would pray for the pilgrim, as they expected the pilgrim to pray for them—and to return with some form of wisdom to share.

Besides the communal support and send-off pilgrims often received, they frequently wore special clothes to identify and perhaps protect themselves. Muslims on the way to Mecca wear white clothing once they have removed their normal attire, which carries marks of social status. Distinctions of

Christian pilgrims on the way to Jerusalem often had cloth crosses blessed and sewn on their hats and cloaks in the presence of the church community.

rank and hierarchy are thus eliminated and all stand as equals before God at the shrine. Buddhist pilgrims on their way to visit the tomb of Kobo Daishi, an eighth-century Buddhist saint, dress as the wandering monk did, in white clothing. For the Japanese, this color symbolizes renewal, and, for those who have completed the pilgrimage, immediate rebirth.

Christian pilgrims on the way to Jerusalem often had cloth crosses blessed and sewn on their hats and cloaks in the presence of the church community. Those on their way to Santiago de Compostela wore scallop shells. To whatever destination, pilgrims often wore broad-brimmed hats to protect themselves from the sun, and carried a staff for the long hours of walking.

Unexpected Helpers

Campbell tells us that in this liminal state, a person is often aided by helpers who appear when most needed. They manifest themselves in many ways. Help might come, for example, from a dream-mentor. In *The Way of a Pilgrim*, the author tells how he was beaten and robbed, but then found help.

His *staretz*, his spiritual guide who had died suddenly sometime before, appears to him in a dream and counsels patience.

> Let this be a lesson to you in detachment from earthly things, for your better advance toward heaven. This has been allowed to happen to you to save you from falling into the mere enjoyment of spiritual things. . . . Take courage and believe that God "will with the temptation provide also a way of escape" (1 Cor 10:13). Soon you will be rejoicing much more than you are now distressed.

"Take courage and believe that God 'will with the temptation provide also a way of escape' (1 Cor 10:13). Soon you will be rejoicing much more than you are now distressed."

The Way of a Pilgrim

With those words, the pilgrim awakens, "feeling my strength come back to me," he says, "and my soul full of light and peace."

Gerald Hughes, a contemporary pilgrim who walked to Jerusalem, tells of help that came to him not in the form of a tangible person, but from the spiritual realm:

> As I walked the roads I often thought of Celtic monks, who wandered through Europe, wondering at the glory of God's creation, preaching the Gospel and founding monasteries. At first they were imaginary figures from the distant past, but they are in God, who is eternal, that is, always in the now, in the God who keeps my legs going along these roads, so those Celtic saints are as near to me as the living, in fact nearer. Why shouldn't St. Patrick cheer me up on the road, just as the waitress cheered me by lighting the candle at the table? Following this line of thought, I found myself talking with these figures from the past and with my own dead relatives and friends, especially with my sister Marie, who died forty years earlier. These conversations became very natural and they could be very helpful in decision-making.

These stories suggest that pilgrims find spiritual r their journey for which they are forever grat dreams that might guide them or departed saints, the people they encounter on the road unexpected ways. In my own travels to the sites of saints, to research their lives and view their landscapes, I am amazed at how much I learn from talking with ordinary people living there. Many have become my guides. I remember especially an Irish nun at a school where I stopped when I was lost. She gave me directions to Killeedy, the home of St. Ita, and even drew me a map. If it had not been for her, I would still probably be going down winding roads.

Re-entry/Return

The third stage, "the return," has to do with bringing back to others what we have learned on our pilgrimage. This can be done in many ways. Certainly our stories, like those Brendan shared with his community, are a gift to those we left behind. We also might give them small tangible gifts to show our love and appreciation for them. All of these can be helpful, but I'm speaking of something much more dramatic, and harder to explain in words: the interior change *in us.* Frequently pilgrims come back to their once familiar surroundings having been changed profoundly by their travels. This is sometimes manifest in the sudden recognition, upon our return, of how much we originally missed or took for granted. T. S. Eliot expresses this beautifully in "Little Gidding," in *Four Quartets:*

> We shall not cease from exploration
> And the end of all our exploring
> Will be to arrive where we started
> And know the place for the first time.

Shirley du Boulay alludes to this experience in *The Road to Canterbury:*

> Eventually we left and drove back to Oxford. For much of the early part of the journey the road runs parallel with the Pilgrims' Way. It felt odd, speeding in the opposite direction, past the places that we had known so recently and explored at such a leisurely pace. The journey that had taken us nearly fourteen days to walk was over in less than three hours. Then home to a pile of post and messages and a broken washing machine. Life must now return to normal, but would it ever be the same again?

She confirms her answer later:

> I had been changed by this pilgrimage, but I do not expect to know how for a long time. Though on this

> Sunday morning I knew the pilgrimage had reached some sort of completion, it had not ended. This symbolic microcosm of the inner journey had to find its resonances with the longer, day-to-day pilgrimage. Perhaps my inability to know when it ended was a precise reflection of its inner parallel. We were resuming our day-to-day lives, our journeys of perpetual pilgrimage. This pilgrimage from Winchester to Canterbury had not ended on arrival any more than life ends with death. But I did feel that I understood better where the sacred place is found.

That sacred place, she implies, is our daily, "ordinary" lives, the place where God speaks, and we respond—or fail to respond. As many people realize, the journey is its own reward, but it always helps us to state, first of all, to ourselves what gift or gifts we have received. Those gifts are frequently the new awarenesses we've come to.

The writer Hannah Green, in the early 1970s, traveled with her husband to the village of Conques in southern France. She was drawn by the story of St. Foy, a young martyr of the fourth century. As a Protestant, she says, she "did not understand the meaning of 'the Communion of Saints,'" but she discovered in Conques new insights into that reality that led her to write *The Little Saint.* She concludes the book with a reference to the spiritual awakening her pilgrimage brought her:

> So I sit in the dark at my typing table, looking out into the night with the wings of my mind hovering over my book of Sainte Foy. Even though it is still only partway to where it will be, and even though I have many times despaired of being able to make it as good as it must be, still it has already brought so much to me as I work to bring it to life and inform it, absorbing knowledge, which in turn is absorbing me and leading me toward Christ the Word.

Green goes on to describe a fabulous dream that contains reference to the beauty of the night, the wonder of the stars:

> A year ago in the fall as we slept in our bedroom under the roof in the "*grand appartement*" above Jack's studio, I dreamed the roof was gone and I could see the night heavens and all the stars in that part of the sky, the southwestern sky, where I would have been looking, asleep in my bed on my back. I could see the stars, and then suddenly from either side, all around, all the stars swooped toward one another, curving, looping with luminous tails like comets, like falling stars in their swiftness. . . . And then the stars formed a cross, which stayed in the sky as if for me. . . . and I knew somehow in my dream that the stars in the form of the cross were

> like Sainte Foy, they were herself turned into stars in the cross of stars . . . , manifesting herself in the here and now of my mind by the will of God: "God is marvelous in His saints." . . . [It] seemed to be Sainte Foy somehow revealed for me, mysteriously there in the starry cross in the heavens, saying, "Don't be afraid. See! See how pretty I am! See what I can do!"

This new appreciation of the communion of saints was Saint Foy's gift to Green, and Green's gift to her readers.

Returning and sharing what we've learned is a gesture of gratitude. As pilgrims of old realized, we must give back something to show our appreciation. Our pilgrim travels are not just for us, but for the community we have left behind: families, friends, and colleagues who might also gain from our experiences. The return is not always easy. And yet, because of what we've gained, it is most worthwhile.

"Pilgrims are poets who create
by taking journeys."

Richard R. Niebuhr

exploring a great spiritual practice

chapterfive

How To Do It—Common Elements of Pilgrimage

"Something to bring back to show you have been there: a lock of God's hair, stolen from him while he was asleep; a photograph of the garden of the spirit."

R. S. Thomas

As our pilgrimages reveal certain common stages, they can also consist of some common elements. Discussing these now may help us prepare for our pilgrim travels, and once we return may help us remember and celebrate them.

Desire

The first element is to identify our hunger, our longing, our desire to visit a certain place. It may be a "sacred site" recognized by a specific spiritual tradition or one that, although seemingly less "religious," may have a great deal of meaning for us personally. An old Jewish Hasidic saying alludes to this: "Carefully observe the way your heart draws you and then choose that way with all your strength."

"Carefully observe the way your **heart** **draws** you and then **choose** that way with all your **strength.**"

Jewish Hasidic saying

Getting in touch with our *deepest* desires means discovering who we are and where God is leading us. What makes a journey sacred is the longing behind it.

Considering this, ask yourself: What places am I drawn to or do I find myself thinking about? Do acquaintances or people in my family or profession encourage me to go to certain sites or countries? Are there places that hold a special fascination for me, possibly from pictures I've seen or movies depicting them? I myself was specifically drawn to Brittany and Galicia not only because of their historical and religious significance, but by two movies I had seen. It was the extraordinary beauty of the landscape depicted in them that pushed me, after years of contemplating that possibility, to finally go on pilgrimage to both places.

Our dreams can reveal our desires. Have you had any dreams in which you find yourself in a strange or unfamiliar place? When and where did it seem to be? What did it evoke in you? Did the dream's images or plot ask you to take some form of travel more seriously? Did it seem to come as an invitation from your ancestors, familial or spiritual, to get to know them better? Dreams often express parts of us that we may need to incorporate more consciously. They frequently have much to teach us about our identity, transformation, or vocation. We need to pay attention to them, for they may express intimations of future pilgrimages we have to make if we are to grow spiritually, creatively.

Our dreams can reveal our desires.

"There is no powerful pilgrimage without love, no memorable journey without the erotic, the presence of Eros animating, enlivening, vitalizing our walks, talks, visits, meals, and conversations."

Phil Cousineau

Our hunger and yearning is really about *eros,* the holy desire for what we do not have, for what we miss, for what will make us whole—and holy; what the ancient Greeks identified as the spiritual power of connection. To go on pilgrimage is to seek connection. We hope for spiritual links with our ancestors, the divine, and our deeper selves. As Phil Cousineau says in *The Art of Pilgrimage,* "There is no powerful pilgrimage without love, no memorable journey without the erotic, the presence of Eros animating, enlivening, vitalizing our walks, talks, visits, meals, and conversations."

With the help of discernment with family and friends, we need to act on our deepest desires. We can make a list of what places we most desire to visit, prioritize them, and then make concrete plans for the pilgrimage.

Motivations

Next, why do we want to go on pilgrimage? People have gone for various reasons. Some set out because their religious traditions encouraged them to do so. Some became pilgrims in order to give thanks for gifts and graces received, or to obtain guidance and divine assistance. Frequently those who were sick, wounded, or maimed sought to be healed, to be cured of the illness or demon that caused them anguish. Still others set out in order to perform acts of penance, seeking forgiveness for past deeds. What is your motivation?

Is it a long-held dream that calls to be fulfilled? Is it grief or guilt around the death of a loved one that seems to invite you to make some sort of recompense? Is it that you want to know your ancestors better? Do you want to learn more about your heroes or saints? Are you motivated because of gratitude? Are you feeling pushed to review the direction of your life? Do you want to explore new territories in order to strengthen your spirituality? Make a list of reasons why you may want to travel on pilgrimage and what you hope to accomplish. This helps clarify conscious and sometimes unconscious motivations.

A Sense of Timing

A third dimension to consider is what time it is for us emotionally, intellectually, psychologically, spiritually. We need to pay attention not so much to chronological time, but to our inner clock. As Chaucer intimates in his *Canterbury Tales*, there are certain times when we particularly long to go on pilgrimage. Sometimes this relates to seasonal changes. In springtime, perhaps, we feel drawn to see a different landscape covered with new flowers and new growth; this may show a desire for inner change or rebirth. Summer with its sunflowers, fuchsias, and lilies may call out to us to appreciate God's abundance, God's nourishment. In the fall, when the leaves of trees are changing to bright colors and fields of corn and wheat have ripened, we may see reminders of our own potentially rich harvest. In winter, we may want to see and enjoy mountains or forests covered with blankets of snow, telling us of the beauty of even the coldest or seemingly most unproductive periods of our lives. All of these *external* manifestations of beauty in creation are related, as we can see, to *interior* movement we should pay attention to.

Theologians Paul Tillich and Henri Nouwen talk about *kairos* time: this Greek word refers to "right time, the time in which something can be done," a time that holds great potential for the discovery of meaning or for healing. In the life of nations, *kairos* time refers to a moment in history that is, Tillich says, pregnant with "a new understanding of the meaning of history and life," a period that often precedes significant historical change. So also in the life of an individual: there are certain times in which we carry the seeds of new birth, new meaning, perhaps a new direction in our lives that we must have the courage to follow. St. Paul speaks of *kairos* time in his second letter to the Corinthians: "Now is the favorable time; this is the day of salvation" (6:2). We need to discern *our* time—and *our* need to act, especially when it comes to pilgrimage.

"Now is the favorable time; this is the day of salvation" (St. Paul). We need to discern *our* time–and *our* need to act, especially when it comes to pilgrimage.

"It is **no coincidence** that many who go on **pilgrimage** are at a **critical stage** of **life**— the transition from teenage years to adulthood, a mid-life point, or at the start of retirement."

Martin Robinson

Martin Robinson, in *Sacred Places, Pilgrim Paths,* writes that "it is no coincidence that many who go on pilgrimage are at a critical stage of life—the transition from teenage years to adulthood, a mid-life point, or at the start of retirement." Pilgrimage uses travel to a particular site as a means of exploring questions that have arisen at these predictable life-transitions. It provides an opportunity to explore them and reach new insights.

If we ignore the sense of timing, we may become, quite literally, sick—sick in body, sick in spirit. The stories of two great spiritual leaders, the twelfth-century Rhineland mystic Hildegard of Bingen, and Black Elk, the famous twentieth-century Oglala Sioux shaman, attest to this. When Hildegard, at the time about 43 years old, refused to listen to her visions, she became physically ill. Only when she was given the courage to act on them did she regain her health—and begin a very creative period in her life. Black Elk was a young boy when he first heard voices, and then had a great vision of his ancestors. Because he was afraid of the voices and the vision, he did not tell anyone about them until he was sixteen years old, when the voices became more insistent, telling him, "It is time! It is time!" All around him he heard that urgent call, "It is time!" even, he says, "from the crows in the day and the coyotes at night." Only when he finally shared what he knew with his tribe did he become well—and give his people, through his vision, the opportunity to do so as well.

So also with us. We need to ask these questions: What "time" is it for me? Where am I age-wise; what possible life-transition am I entering or have I entered? Where am I spiritually? Do I feel a sense of urgency about acting *now*, as if to continue to procrastinate will do some sort of psychological or spiritual harm? Is *now* the acceptable time; is *now* the day of salvation? How might I ultimately profit from taking the risk to set out on a new spiritual adventure?

Surrender: Letting Go

A fourth element of pilgrimage has to do with letting go. This surrender has much to do with simplicity and trust. Simplicity is manifest from the beginning, when we are deciding what to take, and what *not* to take, in our luggage. Besides my wife's admonitions, a saying that I learned from Alcoholics Anonymous reminds me, "Keep it simple, stupid!" Henry David Thoreau affirms this stance when he discusses what he learned at Walden Pond: "Simplify, simplify, simplify!" While you can find out what to bring from material provided by travel agents or pilgrim guides, those going on sacred travel might follow the basic principle that "less is more." The less we bring, the more freedom we will have. Its opposite is also true: the more we carry, the more we will feel the need to protect. St. Francis is right in suggesting that poverty of spirit gives great freedom. Having less to carry or protect, we will be more capable of learning new things and coming to new levels of awareness.

"Less is more."

While on pilgrimage itself, letting go is a prerequisite to a positive experience. We need to learn to let go of expectations and enjoy the ride. We need to keep reminding ourselves there are always hitches; nothing is perfect, there will be days that nothing seems to go right. We can become frustrated, irritable, and totally out-of-sorts, and take it out on anyone who crosses our paths. But this is not the pilgrim spirit. Rather, the pilgrim spirit is about trusting that everything will (eventually) turn out for the best. It is also knowing that some of our worst experiences will be the source of later storytelling, a strengthened sense of solidarity, and even laughter. Again, as Alcoholics Anonymous teaches, "letting go" is directly related to "letting God." We can let go of our need to control everything, and let the divine lead us. This, of course, has to do with trust: trusting that there is a higher

St. Francis is right in suggesting that poverty of spirit gives great freedom. Having less to carry or protect, we will be more capable of learning new things and coming to new levels of awareness.

power who loves us, wants the best for us, and will lead us in the right direction. The sixteenth-century Spanish mystic, John of the Cross, says this another way in *Dark Night of the Soul* (SPCK, 1987):

> Therefore, O spiritual soul, when you see your desire obscured, your affections arid and constrained, and your faculties bereft of their capacity for any interior exercise, be not afflicted by this, but rather consider it a great happiness, since God is freeing you from yourself and taking the work from your hands. . . . God takes your hand and guides you in the darkness, as though you were blind, to an end and by a way which you know not nor could you ever hope to travel with the aid of your own eyes and feet, howsoever good you may be as a walker.

Surrender is not an easy habit to acquire. "Letting go," Shirley du Boulay says in her book about her pilgrimage to Canterbury, is "something I have never been good at." She is not alone. Most of us struggle with this, realizing that it's not only a learned trait but a constant discipline.

We can let go of our need to control everything, and let the divine lead us. This, of course, has to do with trust: trusting that there is a higher power who loves us, wants the best for us, and will lead us in the right direction.

Synchronicity, or Being Led

Another element of pilgrimage has to do with synchronicity, a term Carl Jung uses to describe coincidences that do not appear to be connected, yet turn out to be meaningful. Pilgrims often experience this sense of things coming together for their benefit. It reminds us of Joseph Campbell's stage of liminality, in which a person is both tempted *and helped* on their "road of trials." Help often comes in the form of meeting the right person at the right time who guides us to a place for which we have been searching. This synchronicity many pilgrims equate with the mysterious and often profound experience of *being led.*

Jennifer Westwood writes in *On Pilgrimage: Sacred Journeys around the World,* about an experience she had in the late 1970s. While traveling to the Iranian desert city of Yazd, a flash flood hit the road which she and her family were on. They had been hoping to see the great mosque and its "Towers of Silence" there. At the crossroads where their route was to begin, everyone they met shook their heads and said, "Road closed." They had no idea what to do next, but a stranger came along, someone whom Westwood calls "an angel," and pointed to his gas truck and gestured for them to follow him. "We drove behind him," she says, "for more than a hundred miles, through villages where water blocked the road, going at a run through the wake he created like the Children of Israel at the Red Sea crossing. Villagers turned out to watch. It was crazy, and masterly." When they arrived at their destination, the man "would scarcely take thanks, much less anything more tangible. It was all part of looking out for strangers." Needless to say, Westwood and her family deeply appreciated the angel's compassion and hospitality. They had, quite literally, an experience of being led.

I too have had such occurrences of synchronicity. One of the more memorable took place in Barcelona, Spain, when my friend, Toni, and I were visiting the church called Sagrada Familia (Holy Family). It was designed by the famous architect

Help often comes in the form of meeting the right person at the right time who guides us to a place for which we have been searching. This synchronicity many pilgrims equate with the mysterious and often profound experience of *being led.*

Antoni Gaudi. We had arrived there late in the day, and the church was closed to tourists and pilgrims. I was captivated by its beauty and deeply disappointed that we couldn't enter it. I was also curious about the man who had created it. As we began to walk around it to observe its many towers, statues, and rooms, I asked Toni about Gaudi's life, when he had died, and where he was buried. Toni explained what he knew about this extraordinary architect, but he had no idea where his grave was. As we came to the crypt's entrance, we discovered that the gates were open and local parishioners were entering for the Saturday evening mass. Amazed at our "luck," we went in and wandered from one side-chapel to another. Only when we had made our rounds did we discover that we were directly facing Gaudi's tomb. It was surrounded with candles. Both of us felt we had been led there. I knelt and prayed for Gaudi and thanked God for his wonderful faith and creativity. I also thanked God for bringing us there so unexpectedly.

Synchronicity, as Jung used it, is a psychological term for something that Christians and followers of other spiritual traditions equate with grace, providence, and a loving God who leads people to where they need to go. Not a great deal has been written about this phenomenon on pilgrimage. But for those who do not take for granted mysterious turnings, they soon recognize that something profound is happening as they travel, beyond all their extensive plans and attempts to control the direction or the results. Pay attention, be observant, and write these mysterious coincidences down. It is too easy to forget them and lose touch with the grace that is being manifest through them.

Ritual Dimensions of Pilgrimage

A sixth element is the prayerful . . . and ritual dimensions of pilgrimage. Prayer is *the distinctive activity* of pilgrimage. For pilgrims of all faiths, it is the activity with which one begins his or her sacred travels, the action to which one turns frequently on the road, and the activity with which one ends the journey.

This is helpful not only for the person leaving, but also for the family or

Seven Common Elements of Pilgrimage

- longing
- motivation
- timing
- surrender
- synchronicity
- ritual
- storytelling

community to which one belongs. And it may apply to pilgrimage, but also to any travel we undertake. When my eighteen-year-old son, Daniel, was about to leave for an adventure with a friend in California, we prayed together at the prayer-shrine in my study. Such prayer is a family custom. I lit the candles at the shrine, which contains pictures of our family, those living and dead, and statues of Jesus, Mary, and the saints. On this occasion we prayed for a safe journey, and we gave thanks for our mutual love. I gave him a cross on a chain that I had worn, hugged him, and silently asked God to protect this son. It was a very simple ritual, and it meant a lot to us both. When Daniel returned he told me that he'd worn the chain and cross the whole time he was away, even when he was having the two tattoos painfully imprinted on his biceps!

Every family and community may develop its own prayers and rituals, as people from many different cultures and faiths in the past have done. The Muslim writer Amir Soltani Sheikholeslami, in an article that appeared in the *Harvard Divinity Bulletin* (Spring 2003), gives this description:

> Growing up in Iran, it was impossible to set out on a journey without having my grandmother rush behind us with the family Quran in hand, make us step back into the house, and then circle the Quran above our head while calling upon the Prophet Mohammad and his household to safeguard our travel. Sacred scripture . . . would be puffed around us like a divine fragrance. We would kiss the holy book, and only then could my brothers and I step out of the door.

Another ritual may be to bring along reminders of our loved ones. Besides the pictures of my family I carry in my billfold,

"We need a ritual along the way–placing ashes along a river, flowers on a grave, or engaging in a ritual of that place–so we might truly feel the spirit of the place."

Anthony Lawlor

I always bring two small icons to set up in my room: one of Jesus and the other of St. Michael the Archangel, known as the protector from all evil.

On the pilgrimage itself, prayerful rituals acknowledge and remind us of the sacredness of the journey. As Anthony Lawlor, an American architect, said in a recent interview, "We need a ritual along the way—placing ashes along a river, flowers on a grave, or engaging in a ritual of that place—so we might truly feel the spirit of the place." One such ritual might be lighting candles at the holy sites or shrines we visit, and then kneeling quietly in prayer.

Another prayerful expression as we travel is found in songs sung from the heart. Not only do some pilgrims sing hymns and songs with added devotion while on pilgrimage, but many also unexpectedly find themselves singing or humming certain songs that seem to come unbidden from their unconscious, often from their childhood. I remember especially the great joy at the crypt in Bethlehem where Jesus is said to have been born. Our pilgrim group sang "Away in a Manger," "Silent Night," and "Joy to the World." Many of us cried openly when we linked our own early childhood memories of Christmas with this holy site that has been honored for centuries by faithful Christians.

Prayers in silence and quiet, of course, have their own validity. It is not always necessary to express our prayers out loud. The simplest prayer, perhaps, is that of quiet contemplation. We place ourselves in the presence of the divine. Some pilgrims also find photography an expression of silent contemplation. By looking through the lens and focusing upon some aspect of the landscape or the interior of a grand cathedral, a person comes to new awarenesses that might be missed by trying to take everything in at a glance. Using a camera, as Thomas Merton discovered on his final pilgrimage to Thailand, can be a form of prayer.

Using a camera, as Thomas Merton discovered on his final pilgrimage to Thailand, can be a form of prayer.

There is no *one* way to pray on pilgrimage, and each of us needs to find what is most meaningful to us. The time when I climbed Mount Sinai with its 3700 stone steps, I reached the summit with great exultation—and great exhaustion. Our group contained pilgrims from a variety of Christian denominations and we were divided between two prayerful responses to this accomplishment: Some wanted to sing hymns and some wanted to sit quietly and give thanks. Each of us chose for ourselves the most meaningful way.

Sharing Stories and Celebrating

A seventh element has to do with our return home. Pilgrimage is about reaching one's destination and taking something back: some part of the spirit of a holy place, some positive memories that contain the energy to keep us going, some reminders of our efforts and our having reached an important goal. This idea is expressed powerfully by the Welsh poet R. S. Thomas:

> Something to bring back to show
> you have been there: a lock of God's
> hair, stolen from him while he was
> asleep; a photograph of the garden
> of the spirit. As has been said,
> the point of traveling is not
> to *arrive* but to *return home*
> laden with pollen you shall work up
> into honey the mind feeds on.

As Jacob set up a pillar and poured oil on it to mark the sacred spot where he had dreamed about a ladder and God blessing him and his descendents (Gn 28:10–18), so we all need to honor the revelations we've received on pilgrimage.

We may bring back reminders or mementos from the sacred sites or shrines. This is not about rank commercialism or consumerism, but about remembering and sharing with others where we have been. This has been done over the centuries among most religious traditions. In medieval times a pilgrim could obtain a lead amulet at the tomb of St. Thomas Becket in Canterbury, a scallop shell at Santiago de Compostela, or a palm leaf from the Holy Land (from which the term, "Palmer," derived, denoting a pilgrim who had no home to return to, and traveled continuously from one shrine to another). Some pilgrims attempted to display as many tokens as possible from the holy sites that they had visited, sometimes pinned on their hat or cloak.

Some pilgrims attempted to display as many tokens as possible from the holy sites that they had visited, sometimes pinned on their hat or cloak.

> Some pilgrims bring back amulets, such as those blessed by Buddhist saints that are used for cures in Thailand, or holy water, such as that blessed at the shrine of Our Lady in Lourdes, France.

Today sacred mementos can include statues, carvings, or reliquaries. Some pilgrims bring back amulets, such as those blessed by Buddhist saints that are used for cures in Thailand, or holy water, such as that blessed at the shrine of Our Lady in Lourdes, France. Many pilgrims bring back stones or earth from certain sites, as was done in early medieval times when earth from the tomb of St. Martin of Tours was sent to major churches in France in the sixth and seventh centuries. Pilgrims should bring back something that has meaning for them. Material objects might do, but music also can vividly remind us of important sites. When I travel on pilgrimage, I often bring back compact discs of religious and secular music that help me better understand and appreciate the history and culture of countries and sites I have visited. When I listen to the music (choral music from Russia, pilgrim music from Santiago de Compostela, religious music from Brittany, or ancient chants from Hawaii), I can re-enter the sacred space and landscape I visited and remember with gratitude those sacred places and holy lives.

Pilgrims too, upon their return, often pass around photos or show slides to those who are interested. This can be a meaningful way to share what we saw and what we learned. They provide the opportunity for telling stories. Storytelling deepens the original experience for ourselves, and articulates to others something that they may want to know.

For those who have shared a pilgrimage together, a ritual feast the night before their return home can offer everyone a chance to celebrate and remember all that has been experienced; after their return, another meal to share photos and tell stories is also often greatly appreciated. Members of parishes or religious congregations could share what they experienced on pilgrimage in a more formal way, through lectures or adult forum discussions. We might possibly even join with these communities in a liturgy or ritual of thanksgiving, as many pilgrims have done throughout the centuries. This provides the community an opportunity to participate in a pilgrim's sacred travels.

Finally, it also might be helpful to create some form of shrine or prayer corner at home, some place where quiet reflection can occur. We can encounter once again our saints, ancestors, or heroes, and discover further what they have to teach us about themselves and our own sacred journeys. This remembering with thanks is one of the most important elements of any pilgrimage.

"Uncover what you long for and you will discover who you are."

Phil Cousineau

exploring a great spiritual practice

Conclusion: A Life of Pilgrimage

"The longest **journey**
Is the journey **inwards.**"

Dag Hammarskjöld, Markings

"Let us concern ourselves with things **divine**,
and as pilgrims ever sigh for and desire
our **homeland.**"

St. Columbanus

"And there in front of them was the **star** they
had seen rising; it went forward and halted over
the place where the **child** was."

Matthew 2:9–10

Pilgrimage, as we've seen, has a long and rich history among world religions and spiritual traditions. All of them recognize the practice as a significant resource in the development of one's spirituality. It may be undertaken for a variety of reasons and often consist of recognizable stages and diverse elements. It always has a communal dimension to it, for anyone who sets forth on pilgrimage does not do so for himself or herself alone. There are family and friends who wish us well as we depart, who pray for us while we're away, who welcome us back with open arms. The pilgrims bring back tokens of their love and stories of their travels. Community can also be found while on pilgrimage. The pilgrim frequently discovers a community of fellow-travelers helping each other along the way. And, of course, there are the people, the strangers, the angels who unexpectedly contribute to the quest.

Pilgrimage is a liminoid experience. We leave the familiar behind, enter an in-between state, and return to some degree transformed. According to Joseph Campbell, the stages of the monomyth to which we have compared the pilgrim journey can lead a person to becoming more integrated psychologically, socially, spiritually. From a Buddhist perspective, the pilgrim becomes more "Buddha-like;" from a Jewish or Islamic view, one becomes more holy; from a Christian perspective, one becomes more Christ-like.

Ultimately our sacred travels are about soul-making. We seek a transformation that will better help us not only live well but better prepare us to die well. Pilgrimage is about the discovery that our real pilgrimage is the one we are engaged in each day. As the great Irish missionary, St. Columbanus, reminds us:

> Let us concern ourselves with things divine, and as pilgrims ever sigh for and desire our homeland; for the end of the road is ever the object of the traveler's hopes and desires, and thus, since we are travelers and pilgrims in the world, let us ever ponder on the end of the road, that is of our life, for the end of our roadway is our home.

"My Lord God
I have no idea where I am going.
I do not see the road ahead of me.
I cannot know for certain where it will end.
Nor do I really know myself,
and the fact that I think I am following
your will does not mean
that I am actually doing so.
But I believe that my desire to please you
does in fact please you.
And I hope that I have that desire
in all that I am doing.
I hope that I will never do anything
apart from that desire.
And I know that if I do this
you will lead me by the right road
though I may know nothing about it.
Therefore will I trust you always
though I may seem to be lost
and in the shadow of death.
I will not fear
for you are ever with me,
and you will never leave me
to face my perils alone."

Thomas Merton

Pilgrimages, of course, are not limited to expensive trips abroad. An experience of pilgrimage can happen anywhere, as the early Irish soul friend, Abbess Samanthann, so wisely tells us: "Since God is near to all who call upon him; we are under no obligation to cross the sea. The kingdom of heaven can be reached from every land."

When all is said and done, pilgrimage is about following a star, what we saw earlier as the symbol of the spirit, the spirit of seeking that can lead to the divine—as the star of Bethlehem led the first pilgrims, the Magi, to the Divine Child. The star too is symbolic of the soul, the soul's search for our true home, God. As William Wordsworth expresses it:

> Our birth is but a sleep and a forgetting:
> The Soul that rises with us, our life's Star,
> Hath had else where its setting,
> And cometh from afar:
> Not in entire forgetfulness,
> And not in utter nakedness,
> But trailing clouds of glory do we come
> From God, who is our home. . . .

Besides the star of the Magi, this book has made numerous references to stars: the need to follow our star, as Don Quixote says, "no matter how hopeless, no matter how far." It was this seeking that led Paula to accompany St. Jerome to the Holy Land and settle there herself. Dante speaks of his journey through hell and purgatory to heaven where he found "the Love that moves the sun and all the stars." It was to Santiago de Compostela, meaning "field of the star," to which millions have gone, and continue to go. In recent times, Henry Beston wrote about the sky at night over Cape Cod, and his walking in "the dust of stars" which fill "the night sky in all its divinity of beauty." Hannah Green who went on pilgrimage to Conques in France and stayed, discovered the transforming power of a saint one evening when in a dream she "could see the stars, and then suddenly from either side, all around, all the stars swooped toward one another, curving, looping with luminous tails like comets, like falling stars in their swiftness."

Jack Kerouac, the best-known writer of the "Beat generation" of the 1950s, also makes numerous references to stars in his book, *The Dharma Bums*. He describes himself as "a regular Don Quixote of tenderness" and as a "religious wanderer" in search of "charity and kindness and humility and zeal and neutral tranquillity and wisdom and ecstasy." With his friend, Japhy Ryder, he searches "to find the ecstasy of the stars," to incorporate the wisdom of Buddha with the truths of his earlier Christianity. Like Christ, Kerouac says, Buddha taught him, "Compassion is the guide-star." Travelling on pilgrimage, as the Russian "holy fools" had done, Kerouac describes his journeys from San Francisco to the high Sierras and, finally, to Desolation Peak in Washington State. There on the peak, alone, Kerouac reflects on his journey, and his anticipated return:

> It was Japhy who had advised me to come here and now though he was seven thousand miles away in Japan answering the meditation bell . . . he seemed to be standing on Desolation Peak by the gnarled old rocky trees certifying and justifying all that was here. "Japhy," I said out loud, "I don't know when we'll meet again or what'll happen in the future, but Desolation, Desolation, I owe so much to Desolation, thank you forever for guiding me to the place where I learned all. Now comes the sadness of coming back to cities and I've grown two months older and there's all that humanity of bars and burlesque shows and gritty love, all upsidedown in the void. God bless them, but Japhy you and me forever we know, O ever youthful, O ever weeping." Down on the lake rosy reflections of celestial vapor appeared, and I said, "God, I love you" and looked up to the sky and really meant it. "I have fallen in love with you, God. Take care of us all, one way or the other."

Kerouac's prayer is mine as well—to God, and to you, the reader. Take care of yourself. Know that you are loved, and be compassionate toward others. I wish you the best as your sacred journey continues to unfold, and I bless you with the words of an Irish farewell prayer:

> May the stars light your way
> and may you find the interior road.
> Forward!

exploring a great spiritual practice

40 Famous Pilgrims

Abraham

Earliest recorded pilgrim, revered by the three great monotheistic religions of Judaism, Christianity, and Islam. Four thousand years ago, Abraham, at the age of 75, traveled with his wife **Sarai** from Ur in Mesopotamia to Canaan and Egypt, following God's call. In certain Christian hagiographies of the Celtic saints, Abraham is referred to as the predecessor of their own pilgrim journeys.

Alighieri, Dante (1265–1321)

Author of *The Divine Comedy,* in which he portrays himself as a pilgrim, led through hell and purgatory by the Roman writer, Virgil, and through paradise by Beatrice, his muse. The entire work presumes every person's life is a sacred journey through trials and darkness to God.

Arculf

Seventh-century bishop from Gaul who went on pilgrimage to the Holy Land in the 680s. The description of this prelate's visits over a nine-month period to holy sites in Jerusalem, Nazareth,

Bethlehem, and Mount Tabor, is found in a book written by Adomnan at St. Columba's monastery on Iona, off the west coast of Scotland.

Ashoka

In the Sanskrit poem, *Ashokavadana*, this emperor who ruled from about 274–232 B.C.E. united almost all of India under his power. A convert to Buddhism, he visited all the major sites of the Buddha's life with his spiritual master, the monk Upagupta. Ashoka is considered the earliest Buddhist pilgrim.

Basil the Great (c. 330–79)

Journeyed from Cappadocia in Turkey to visit the desert with his brother **Gregory of Nyssa** (c. 330–395) and their sister **Macrina** (c. 327–79). Basil and Gregory, along with Gregory Nazianzus, are called the "Cappadocian Fathers," who as theologians had a major impact on Christianity. Basil, in particular, founded monasteries in Cappadocia, and left a monastic rule that is still followed by monks in the Eastern Orthodox Church. Macrina also founded a monastic community.

Benjamin of Tudela

A twelfth-century Jewish rabbi who during the 1160s traveled to Palestine from his home in Spain. He left an account of his journey that took him through Italy, Greece, Constantinople, and the Middle East to the Holy Land, and from there to Baghdad and Persia before he returned via Egypt, Sicily, and Germany.

Biscop, Benedict (628–689)

Nobleman from Northumbria in England who became a monk and founded the abbeys of Wearmouth and Jarrow. From his five pilgrimages to Rome he brought back important art and books for the abbey churches and scriptoria. He also visited Lerins, a small island off the south coast of France, and brought the Benedictine rule from there to Britain, which had a major influence on the development of English and later Anglican spirituality. The Venerable Bede writes admiringly of Biscop in his *Lives of the Abbots of Wearmouth and Jarrow*.

Basho, Matsuo (1644–1694)

Japan's most celebrated haiku master was born into a Samurai family and became known as a poet when he was quite young. Basho trained in Zen meditation under the priest Butcho, whose hermitage he visited in his pilgrimage to the north. As a Buddhist pilgrim, Basho spent the last ten years of his life going on a number of journeys in search of ecstasy. He wrote about his experience in poems, journals, and the book, *A Narrow Road to the Far Places,* which has been described as one the most masterly and evocative travel books ever written.

Brendan the Navigator (c. 486–578)

An Irish saint whose story of his search for the Promised Land became one of the most popular writings of the medieval and late medieval period. It even influenced Columbus in his search for the "New World." The work depicts Brendan as a holy monk who is collaborative in his decision-making and compassionate in his travels. As a story, it reflects many aspects of Celtic spirituality, both pagan and Christian, as well as the genre of literature about voyagers called *immram.*

Burton, Sir Richard (1821–1890)

The best-known of all Christians to visit Mecca. This British explorer, disguised as a Muslim pilgrim, traveled to the holy city in 1853 and kept a journal of what he saw. His three-volume work was published as *Pilgrimage to Mecca and Al-Medinah,* which was recognized not only as a great adventure narrative, but also a classic commentary on Muslim life and manners, especially on the annual pilgrimage.

Cassian, John (c. 360–435)

One of the most influential writers on the development of Christian spirituality in both East and West. Around 380, he traveled with his friend **Germanus** to the holy places of Palestine. In Bethlehem, they joined a monastery near the cave of the Nativity, and remained there for several years, sharing a common cell. They then moved on to Egypt where, for the next fifteen years or so they lived with various desert hermits who taught them by their words, but even more importantly by their example. When Cassian moved to Marseilles in Gaul, he founded a double monastery where he wrote *Conferences* and *Institutes,* two works that contributed immensely to the rise of monasticism in the Celtic Church and the Middle Ages.

Charlemagne (c. 742–814)

The greatest of the Frankish kings who was crowned in Rome by the Pope as Holy Roman Emperor in 800. He went as a pilgrim to Rome four times. In his court in Aachen, Germany, he gathered leading scholars and teachers, including Alcuin of York, to reform the church and its liturgies, and improve the education of his people. Charlemagne himself passed a series of decrees stating that pilgrims must not be denied shelter or water, and that bishops must give hospitality to the poor and to pilgrims.

Columbanus (c. 543–615)

Irish missionary, who left in 590 with **St. Gall** (d. 630) and other monks to evangelize the European continent. They sailed to Brittany and then made their way inland to Frankish Gaul. While St. Gall stayed behind in 612 to found St. Gallen in Switzerland, Columbanus founded the important monasteries of Annegray and Luxeuil in Burgundy, and Bobbio in Italy, where he died. Columbanus compares life to a pilgrimage in his writings. He is considered one of the founders of modern Europe, and one of the first to journey as a pilgrim from Ireland for the sake of Christ. Pilgrims today can pray in Bobbio at his tomb, a beautifully-carved white marble sarcophagus, or at the grand medieval church with his relics in Luxeuil. The Abbey of St. Gall in St. Gallen became a major pilgrim site in the Middle Ages.

Egeria

A late fourth-century nun, probably from that Celtic region of northwestern Spain called Galicia, who in the 380s traveled to the Sinai and Palestine as well as Constantinople and Edessa. She described four journeys in a journal. She is constantly enthusiastic about what she does and sees, and provides us with a clearer understanding of Holy Week liturgical services and the churches in Jerusalem.

Erasmus, Desiderius (c. 1469–1536)

A Christian humanist who in about 1512 and 1514 made pilgrimages to Walsingham and Canterbury, the two pre-eminent English shrines, and wrote critically of his experience in his *Colloquy* in a chapter entitled "The Religious Pilgrimage." He derides the profusion of golden tombs, candlesticks, and images "when our brothers and sisters . . . are ready to die from hunger and thirst."

Fabri, Felix

A Dominican friar from Ulm, Germany. He visited the Holy Land twice in the 1480s. He wrote of his travels in a long work, *Evagatorium in Terrae Sanctae* [*Wandering in the Holy Land*], which was read by his brother monks as well as a much wider German audience. It is considered a classic in pilgrimage writings; it combines a description of the interior life of the pilgrim and the sights and sounds of the outer journey.

Fa-hsien

In about 400 C.E., this Chinese monk made the long journey to India, visiting the shrines and holy places of Buddha. Accompanied by other Buddhist monks, he traveled for fourteen years in the Indian subcontinent as far as Sri Lanka. In his written account, he often remarks on the works and legends of Ashoka, and he reveals many of the qualities of Buddhist spirituality.

Francis of Assisi (1181–1226)

Founder of the Franciscan Order. He was raised in a wealthy family, became dissatisfied with his life, and determined to devote himself to the poor. On a pilgrimage to Rome, Francis was moved to compassion for the beggars at St. Peter's Basilica, and returned to Assisi where he publicly disassociated himself from his father. He then started his new life in earnest, ministering to lepers and repairing the church of San Damiano. Eventually others began to follow him. In 1214–15, he traveled on pilgrimage through southern France and Spain, hoping to convert the Moors. In 1219, he made a preaching tour through Eastern Europe and Egypt, and in 1220 went as a pilgrim to Jerusalem, where he spent a year. Franciscans after him became guardians of numerous pilgrim sites in the Holy Land, where many still minister today.

Gerald of Wales (c. 1145–1223)

One of the most dynamic churchmen of the Middle Ages. Gerald was a member of one of the leading Norman families involved in the invasion of Ireland in the twelfth century. He traveled as a pilgrim to Ireland in 1183 for the first time, and then again, accompanying Henry II, in 1185; in 1188 he visited Wales with Baldwin, Archbishop of Canterbury. Gerald left wonderful accounts of those journeys with astute and at times highly critical commentaries about whom and what he saw. His lifelong ambition was to become bishop of St. David's in Wales, a goal he never achieved, although his body rests in the cathedral there, a site visited by thousands of pilgrims each year.

Helena (c. 255–330)

Mother of the Emperor Constantine. Despite her advanced age, she visited Palestine in 326 where she had basilicas built on the Mount of Olives and at Bethlehem. According to fourth-century writers, Sulpicius Severus, Ambrose, and Rufinus, Helena discovered the cross on which Jesus had been crucified. There is a special chapel dedicated to her in the Church of the Holy Sepulcher, where a statue of her is visible to the modern pilgrim.

Hsuan-tsang

The most famous and most influential of all Chinese pilgrims. He traveled to India where he lived from 629–645 C.E. Hsuan-tsang not only wrote an extensive account of his pilgrimage in twelve books, the *Si-Yu-Ki* ("Records of the Western World"), but as soon as he died, he became the subject of a hagiographical writing by two of his students. This biography dwells in detail on his trip to India, turning it into a paradigmatic pilgrimage. As the myth of Ashoka became the model for Buddhist pilgrimage within India, that of Hsaun-tsang became the paradigm for pilgrimage to India from China.

Ibn Battuta (b. 1304)

A theologian born in Tangier who devoted much of his life to journeying through Asia and Africa. He described significant aspects of the Muslim world. Again and again, he returned to Mecca, so much so that he became known as the "Traveler of Islam."

Ignatius of Loyola (1491–1556)

Founder of the Jesuits. Throughout his autobiography this Spanish mystic identifies himself as a pilgrim. Before settling in Rome during his later years, he traveled to numerous holy Christian shrines, including Palestine in 1523. His *Spiritual Exercises* encourages people to travel in prayer to the holy sites associated with Jesus, and imagine with all their senses what it is like to be with him on his spiritual journey through the passion, death, and resurrection.

Jerome (331–420), Paula (347–404), and Eustochium (370–c. 419)

These three friends—the famous early Christian theologian and writer, the wealthy Roman widow, and her daughter—traveled together as pilgrims to various sites in the Holy Land. They finally settled in Bethlehem, where Jerome was in charge of a men's monastery and the two women led a women's convent. Together they welcomed refugees fleeing the fall of Rome in 410 C.E., as well as pilgrims who were seeking shelter.

Kempe, Margery (c. 1373–1440)

After she received several visions, she and her husband John went as pilgrims to Canterbury. In 1413, Margery went alone to the Holy Land. Upon her return, she went to Norwich to seek guidance from Julian of Norwich, the anchoress, who seems to have listened compassionately. Margery also visited Santiago de Compostela in 1417, and Norway in 1433. *The Book of Margery Kempe* describes her pilgrim travels and her mystical relationship with Jesus.

Kerouac, Jack (1922–1969)

American writer of Breton origins who is associated with the "Beat Generation" of the 1950s–60s. He is best known for two works that reflect his passion for pilgrimage, his search for ecstasy (like the Buddhist pilgrim, Matsuo Basho), and his longing for God: *On the Road* (1957) and *The Dharma Bums* (1958).

Luther, Martin (1483–1546)

A monk and a professor of theology at the University of Wittenberg in Germany. Luther went on pilgrimage to Rome in 1510. In his *Address to the Christian Nobility of the German Nation* (1521), Luther states that the practice of pilgrimage is an occasion for sin, and that secular and religious leaders should persuade people to stay home where they belong and spend their money and time on their families and the poor.

Mary of Egypt (fifth century)

This saint, after a career as an actress and prostitute in Alexandria, traveled by ship to Jerusalem with other pilgrims. At the Church of the Holy Sepulcher, she was stopped from entering, as if by an invisible shield. There, at the threshold, she surrendered her life to Christ, then fled into the desert east of Palestine to expiate her sins. For forty-seven years she lived as a hermit until the monk Zossima found her and brought her communion before she died. She is honored by both western and eastern Christians.

Merton, Thomas (1915–1968)

One of the most influential spiritual writers of the twentieth-century. Merton authored more than forty books of poetry, essays, and religious writings. He was a Trappist monk at Gethsemani, Kentucky, for much of his adult life. In 1968, he flew to Bangkok, Thailand, on a pilgrimage to visit some of the great Buddha statues and for a conference on eastern and western monasticism at which he was to be a main presenter. There he died tragically, electrocuted by a faulty fan as he stepped from a shower.

Muhammad (570–632)

Founder of Islam. Muhammad was an orphan at an early age and developed a compassionate attitude toward all who suffered, as well as a deep desire to help the poor and weak. He reached a time in his life of severe anguish and of revelation, when the angel Gabriel came to him in a cave and admonished him to proclaim the message that God "is the Most Generous" (Quran 96:1–3). Following his vision of one God whose name is Allah, he went on to unite a desert people who had been primarily animists (they believed in many gods and spirits). He traveled to Medina in 622 and returned to Mecca eight years later and became the inspiration for all of his pilgrim-followers.

Picaud, Aymery

Author of *Pilgrim's Guide to Santiago.* Picaud was a monk from Parthenay-le-Vieux, thirty miles to the west of Poitiers, France. He made a pilgrimage to Santiago and wrote of his experience around 1140–1150. For centuries his was the primary resource for those travelling to Santiago de Compostela.

Russian Pilgrim

Anonymous pilgrim who wrote the classic work, *The Way of a Pilgrim.* He describes his journey through Russia and Siberia during the mid-nineteenth century, when he visited monasteries and the shrines of the saints while learning to "pray without ceasing." His pilgrimage leads him to a wise elder, a *staretz,* who teaches him the Jesus Prayer, an uninterrupted mantra-like invocation of the name of Jesus. The original manuscript came into the hands of a monk on Mount Athos in the nineteenth century and was first published in 1884. It expresses well basic characteristics of Russian Orthodox spirituality, and shows the passage from searching to find a spiritual mentor to becoming one.

exploring a great spiritual practice

40 Famous Holy Places

• Amsterdam, Holland

Amsterdam has a wealth of places that millions of tourists, sightseers, and pilgrims visit each year. Some of the world's greatest landscape artists came from Holland, and many of their works are on display at the Rijksmuseum. The paintings of Rembrandt (1606–69), called "the painter of humanity," have inspired generations—not only his portraits, but his Biblical and historical scenes as well. Vincent van Gogh was one of those so inspired, and the largest display of his works can be found in the Van Gogh Museum. Anne Frank's House, in which she and her family hid from 1942–1944, before the Nazis shipped them to concentration camps, is a pilgrimage site for people of all religious beliefs. To stand in the tiny room where she wrote her poignant diary is, for many, a sacred moment.

• Assisi, Italy

Four to five million pilgrims visit the home of St. Francis and St. Clare annually. Assisi is revered not only by Christians, but also by Buddhists, Muslims, animists, and New-Agers alike. The Basilica of St. Francis is especially worth visiting, frescoed as it is from top to bottom by leading artists. Giotto's works, in particular, which tell the story of Francis's life, are amazing. Francis's tomb is in the crypt, while St. Clare's is in the Basilica that bears her name.

• Avila, Spain

Avila is the home of St. Teresa, one of the greatest Christian reformers and mystics. Pilgrims who stay within this walled city can experience firsthand what late medieval Spanish Christianity was like. They can also understand how St. Teresa conceived the image for her classic *The Interior Castle*, which describes stages of the mystical path. One site which every pilgrim should visit is the Convent of the Incarnation where St. Teresa lived for thirty years, where her friend, St. John of the Cross, frequently visited her, and where the two are said to have levitated while at prayer.

• Barcelona, Spain

Barcelona is home to the famous and spectacular church dedicated to the Holy Family. It is a work in progress, begun in 1882 and set to be completed in 2022. The architect Antoni Gaudi designed it. Statues and towers seem both ancient and futuristic, with animals, angels, and saints interwoven throughout, like a page from the Book of Kells. The color of its exterior changes as the sun, moon, and stars cross the skies over Barcelona.

• Borobudur, Java

Borobudur is the largest Buddhist monument in the world. Built around 800, it is believed to have taken ten thousand men one hundred years to construct. Borobudur is located on a hilltop and is built in the form of a step pyramid, comprising six rectangular stories, three circular terraces, and a central dome that forms the summit. Many pictorial and ornamental relief panels tell stories from the Buddha's life.

• Canterbury, England

After Jerusalem, Rome, and Santiago, the major medieval Christian pilgrim site was Canterbury, where Archbishop Thomas Becket was killed by soldiers of King Henry II in 1170. Within days of Becket's martyrdom, pilgrims began to travel to Canterbury, and they have not stopped since, even though King Henry VIII had the shrine desecrated and the relics dispersed during his reign. Chaucer, who probably visited Canterbury as a pilgrim, immortalized this site through his writings.

Chartres, France

Chartres Cathedral is the world's most complete and most beautiful example of Gothic art and architecture, built on a site where Celtic druids gathered annually. Although one can see displayed the treasured relic of Mary's "sacred tunic," what probably affects the pilgrim most is the interior of the church itself, lit by sunlight flooding through its jewel-colored stained-glass windows. A labyrinth, at the center of the nave and symbolic of the pilgrim's path to God, provides a rich experience to those who walk it. This medieval cathedral, like others, was built to symbolize the Heavenly Jerusalem (cf. Rev. 21) awaiting pilgrims at the end of their life-journeys.

Czestochowa, Poland

More than a hundred thousand pilgrims are drawn to this industrial town in southwest Poland each year. They come to honor the shrine of the icon of the Black Madonna, Our Lady of Czestochowa, whose exact origin is unknown, although it probably dates from around the fifth century. Many people travel from Warsaw at dawn on August 6 so that, by walking 180 miles, they can arrive nine days later on the eve of the Assumption, the most important Marian feast in the liturgical year.

• Downpatrick, Northern Ireland

Cathedral Hill in Downpatrick has been a place where Christians have worshipped for centuries, almost as long as Christianity has been in Ireland. St. Patrick is said to have begun his missionary work in this area. He landed nearby in about 432 at Saul, where a small church stands today, and went on to Armagh. Patrick's actual grave is probably located underneath Down Cathedral, although a spurious memorial stone with his name lies in the nearby cemetery.

• Einsiedeln, Switzerland

Hundreds of thousands of pilgrims each year visit the Benedictine monastery in Einsiedeln where the Black Madonna is honored. This madonna figure, like the Buddha, has a face that invites serenity, healing, and contemplation. The most beautiful of all the black madonnas in Europe, with the possible exception of Montserrat's in Spain, Einsiedeln's represents the sacred feminine, which too often and for too long has been repressed and undervalued. Kneeling or sitting before her and the black child she holds in her arms, the pilgrim can find peace. Though some commentators say that these madonnas are black because smoke from candles over the centuries has darkened them, they quite obviously were originally created that way—people, artisans, and mystics were valuing the beauty and creativity of darkness.

• Ephesus, Turkey

In ancient times, the city was associated with Artemis, a goddess of hunting and abundance; in Christian times it was associated with St. John, the beloved disciple of Jesus, and Jesus' mother, Mary. Ephesus is where St. John wrote the fourth gospel of the New Testament, and where Mary lived after Jesus' death and resurrection. From late antiquity on, pilgrims desiring to be near the two people who were closest to Jesus visited the Church of St. John where the evangelist was buried, and the Church of St. Mary, as well as the house where Mary lived and possibly died at the age of sixty-four.

• Glastonbury, England

The small town of Glastonbury is in Somerset, southwest England. According to legend, Joseph of Arimathea, Jesus' uncle who provided his tomb for his dead nephew, journeyed here, perhaps bringing with him the Holy Grail. Glastonbury with its Tor (an Old English word for "hill") overlooking it, has rich Celtic and Arthurian associations. Its first Christian monastery was founded by Irish or Welsh missionaries, and it went on to become one of the wealthiest and most respected monasteries in all of England, even claiming to possess the bodies of Arthur and Guinevere. Thousands of pilgrims and seekers continue to come here each year, especially in late June or early July when Anglicans, Catholics, and Orthodox believers flock to the monastic ruins to pray.

• Iona, Scotland

Originally inhabited by Celtic druids, this island off the northwestern coast of Scotland became famous for its association with St. Columba who arrived there in 563. He set forth from Iona to convert the pagan Picts. Today the ecumenical Iona Community welcomes pilgrims from around the world to participate in its liturgies and its revived Christian Celtic spiritual practices on the site where Columba's monastery once stood.

• Istanbul, Turkey

In the city that the Roman emperor Constantine named after himself (Constantinople), he built one of the greatest Christian churches of all time, Hagia Sophia (Holy Wisdom). Crowned with a huge dome and containing the relics of numerous saints, this edifice became a major pilgrim destination for Christians from Asia, Russia, and Europe. Crusaders looted it of its treasures, however, and when the Muslim Turks took over the city, they transformed it into a mosque. In 1935, Hagia Sophia was turned into a museum. Pilgrims enjoy its rich history and newly-restored mosaics.

• Jerusalem, Israel

This city is revered by three great religions, Judaism, Christianity, and Islam. The holiest Christian church, the Church of the Holy Sepulcher, is built on the site of Jesus' crucifixion. It contains a special chapel honored as the tomb where Jesus' body lay before his resurrection.

There is credible evidence that this tomb, found in 325 C.E. under a Roman temple in Jerusalem, has a valid claim to be the tomb of Jesus. From late antiquity on through the middle ages to our own time, pilgrims have sought out this holy site. Many have left records of their pilgrimage to it and of their tears of awe and gratitude upon seeing it. The Dome of the Rock is Jerusalem's most celebrated Muslim shrine. It dominates the entire Old City. Beneath it stands the great Holy Rock which is also sacred to Jews and Christians. Muslims believe that the dome is an *axis mundi,* marking the center of the world where heaven and earth meet. Pilgrims can go below the rock into a large cave where, legend says, Abraham offered his son, Isaac, to God, and where, Muslims believe, Muhammad began his night journey to heaven. A shrine near the cave's entrance contains relics of the Prophet. The entire edifice stands on the site where Judaism's Temple of Solomon once stood. This makes the place a source of much contention and outright bloodshed. The only access Jews have to it is the Wailing Wall, where thousands of Jewish pilgrims come daily to pray.

• Kizhi, Russia

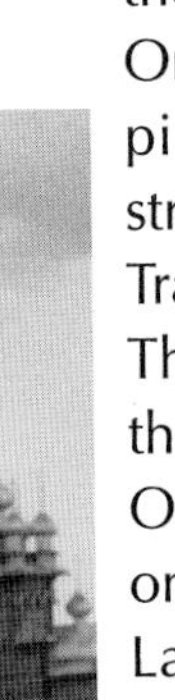

Kizhi is a holy island in the Onega Lake, located in the territory of present-day Republic of Karelia, in the northern part of Russia. Loved by Russian Orthodox Christians and all those who visit as pilgrims, it has a configuration of wooden structures, including the famous Church of the Transfiguration, crowned with twenty-one cupolas. This unique church, built in 1714 without a nail, is the most beautiful ecclesial structure of Old Rus. Other smaller churches of wood dot the island, one of which, the Church of the Resurrection of Lazarus, is considered to be the oldest preserved monument of Russia.

• Lindisfarne, England

In the seventh century, the Celtic missionary St. Aidan brought Christianity to northern England from Iona. He founded the monastery of Lindisfarne in 635. It was here that one of the most beloved saints, Cuthbert, later lived and ministered as abbot, bishop, spiritual guide, and hermit. From here too Lindisfarne's monks evangelized much of the area, as well as Scotland. Though Cuthbert's remains now rest in Durham Cathedral, pilgrims by the thousands, especially during the summer months, travel to this Holy Isle, which is cut off from the mainland by the ebb and flow of tides.

• Lourdes, France

In February, 1858, Bernadette Soubirous, a poor, illiterate fourteen-year-old French girl, began seeing apparitions of the Blessed Virgin Mary in a grotto near her home town. Her eighteen visions over a period of five months transformed Lourdes into the most frequented place of Christian pilgrimage in the world. Drawn to the site where a miraculous spring gushed forth, pilgrims today attempt to wash in its waters or be blessed by them. Lourdes is a place of physical, spiritual, and emotional healing, giving hope to those for whom all other remedies have failed.

• Mecca, the Republic of Saudi Arabia

If they are financially able, Muslims are required to go to Mecca at least once in their lifetimes. Mecca is considered the holiest city in Islam, the site where Muhammad was born and lived until 622, when he was forced to flee to Medina. Ten years later, upon his return, Mecca became the site of his last pilgrimage. Today pilgrims first visit the sacred mosque, and then circle the Ka'ba (the holy black stone) seven times counterclockwise and kiss it. The pilgrimage continues as followers go the well of Aamzam where they drink water before walking seven times between the hills of Safa and Marwa. At Arafat, where Muhammad preached his last sermon, they pray until sunset. The next day, they sacrifice an animal at Eid-ul-Adha and throw stones at pillars, symbolizing their rejection of evil. Finally they return to Mecca to circle the Ka'ba once more.

• Mexico City, Mexico

Millions of pilgrims visit the Basilica of Our Lady of Guadalupe where an Indian peasant named Juan Diego received apparitions of Mary on Tepeyac Hill, now a suburb of Mexico City, in 1531, ten years after the Spanish had devastated the Aztecs. Mary appeared as a native woman, with dark features, and spoke in Nahuatl, the Aztec language. Her message was not of bloodshed but of love. The modern basilica built in the 1970s displays the mysterious cloak with its picture of the Virgin on it, which Juan took to a skeptical bishop to prove his case for constructing a church on the site. Juan Diego, declared a saint by John Paul II, is buried in the old basilica. There are always large crowds of pilgrims at the shrine, most especially on the feast day of December 12, the anniversary of the second apparition of Our Lady to Juan Diego.

• Montserrat, Spain

The shrine of the Black Madonna of Montserrat is one of the most important places of pilgrimage in Spain. Visitors can climb the mountain or take a cable car. The Benedictine community at the shrine offers warm hospitality. Monsterrat's Black Madonna and Child are exquisite expressions of divine compassion, and pilgrims climb the stairs behind the altar to kiss her extended hand which bears the world.

• Mont St. Michel, France

Since the eighth century, Christian pilgrims have been visiting this small island off the coast of Normandy where the Archangel Michael is said to have appeared in 708. It was one of the great centers of pilgrimage in medieval Christianity. Today, a Benedictine abbey crowns the summit and provides visitors with a spectacular view of the surrounding beaches and countryside. The island, like Lindisfarne in northern England, is totally surrounded by the sea at high tide. The devotion of Joan of Arc to St. Michael may have originated with the stories she heard as a child about this famous holy site.

• Mount Athos, Greece

One of the holy mountains of humankind is Mount Athos, established by a Christian monk, Athanasius, in the ninth century. The peninsula in northern Greece on which Mount Athos rises contains twenty monasteries and numerous small hermitages of various Orthodox Christian faiths: Greek, Russian, Serbian, and Bulgarian. It is by far the largest and most important community of Eastern Orthodox monks in the world, and it has a long and rich history of spirituality. Many Russian Orthodox spiritual leaders studied there, and took what they learned back to their fellow Christians. About fifteen hundred monks live there now, worshipping, studying, and contemplating the mystery of God. Each monastery has a guestmaster who looks after pilgrims who are allowed to stay for four days (an extension is often possible).

• Mount Fuji, Japan

Mount Fuji is sixty miles from Tokyo. It is a holy mountain dear to the Japanese Shinto followers as well as Buddhists. Its peak, covered with snow in winter, is awe-inspiring. Entire families of pilgrims climb it in a series of ten clearly-marked stages that, if calculated rightly, can lead to the attainment of the summit at dawn. As the first rays of light appear, thousands of pilgrims all over the mountain raise their arms and shout, "Bonsai!" Mount Fuji is considered not only the personification of a *kami*, or spirit of the place, but also the home of a goddess.

• Mount Kailash, Tibet

Located in the Himalaya Mountains near Lake Manasarovar, Mount Kailash is one of Tibetan Buddhism's most visited holy sites. Hindus, Jains, and other religious groups also go there. It rises more than twenty-two thousand feet above sea level, and it is surrounded by the caves of legendary lamas [teachers] Milarepa, Padmasambhava, and Atisha. For Buddhists, this holy mountain represents a gigantic mandala, "the Mandala of the Highest Bliss," considered to be the abode of Buddha and many Bodhisattvas. To traverse its slopes, for the pilgrim, is to experience a passage through sacred space, a voyage through life and death.

• Norwich, England

Norwich is the home of Julian, the famous fourteenth-century English anchoress (a woman dedicated to solitude). Julian of Norwich is one of the most lovable medieval Christian mystics. Her theology of God was compassionate and androgynous (she addressed Jesus as "Mother"), and her ministry was broad and accepting. Margery Kempe, on pilgrimage, came to her for advice. Today pilgrims from all over the world visit her cell attached to a church. This cell originally had two windows: one that opened to the church, where she could receive the eucharist, and the other opened to the busy street, where she could dispense spiritual wisdom. Her life affirms the importance of solitude and contemplation, and the two windows remind Christians of the importance of the eucharist and spiritual guidance.

• Paris, France

Montmartre, the region of Paris that was the site of Montmartre Abbey, became the home of numerous artists in the nineteenth century, such as Corot, Delacroix, Degas, Renoir, Cezanne, Manet, Toulouse-Lautrec, and Vincent van Gogh. Today Montmartre square is popular with painters, portrait artists, and caricaturists, who, with the many cafes and cabarets, create a joyous, pilgrim atmosphere. Nearby, on the highest of Montmartre hills is Sacre Coeur; its magnificent white dome overlooks the city. Thousands of pilgrim groups gather within its walls to celebrate the eucharist, or outside on the steps to play guitars, sing, and dance. God's spirit is everywhere in Montmartre and Sacre Coeur, a spirit of love, creativity, and happiness.

Poitiers, France

Poitiers is the home of St. Hilary of Poitiers, who wrote one of the earliest theological works on the Holy Spirit. His church, first built in the sixth century, is a major pilgrimage site. The city of Poitiers has numerous churches besides his, including a fourth-century baptistery, that is one of the oldest Christian buildings in France. The most beautiful Christian structure, however, is Notre Dame La Grande, a pilgrim church whose interior reflects Islamic designs that originated with the Crusaders. A statue of the Virgin stands in the sanctuary, and one can see behind it where medieval pilgrims walked and touched sacred relics. The church was built in the eleventh or twelfth century.

• Saint-Malo, France

This walled city was founded by a Welsh pilgrim, St. Malo, who is said to have been a disciple of the Irish voyager Brendan. It was occupied by the Nazis during World War II and was almost totally destroyed by Allied bombers in the closing days of the war. The city was miraculously rebuilt stone by stone. One of its most charming wonders is the Cathedral of St. Vincent, which has beautiful stained-glass windows and a modern altar of green and gold with symbols of the four evangelists. Considering the destruction of the city, it is significant that this church is dedicated to world peace.

• St. Catherine's Monastery, the Sinai

This monastery, in a narrow valley below Mount Sinai where Moses received the ten commandments, was founded in the sixth century. This makes it the oldest continuous Christian community in the world.

It is named after the fourth-century martyr, scholar, and spiritual teacher, St. Catherine of Alexandria, who was placed on a broken wheel (which became her symbol) and beheaded. The main church in the monastery contains her relics as well as a large collection of mosaics and icons that are some of the earliest depictions of Jesus, Mary, and the saints. St. Catherine's welcomes people throughout the year, although the best times to visit are April and October when it is not too hot. A hostel next to the monastery provides simple meals and overnight lodging.

• Santiago de Compostela, Spain

This cathedral town is named after St. James "the Great" (brother of St. John the Evangelist), whom St. Jerome, among others, said had been a missionary to Spain. After his death in Jerusalem in 44, James' bodily remains were brought here and then evidently largely forgotten—until the "discovery" of his tomb about 820, just about the time of the Muslim invasions. Soon pilgrims were flocking to his grave, praying for help in their personal lives and also for help against the Moors. "Compostela" means "field of the star," a designation based upon the story that a heavenly light had shown where James' tomb had been. St.

James himself was linked with pilgrimage, and statues of him are found throughout Europe, especially in Brittany and Spain. Pilgrimages to Santiago became extremely popular when sites in the Holy Land were more difficult to reach, due to the Muslim capture of the Holy Land. Instead of traversing dangerous territory, pilgrims went to holy sites in Europe to pray and receive indulgences. After Jerusalem and Rome, Santiago was the most visited shrine. The scallop shell, which later became identified so closely with pilgrim dress, originated here in Galicia.

• Shwe Dagon, Rangoon, Myanmar

The Shwe Dagon is one of the most venerated pagodas in Asia and one of the largest of its type. It was built 2,500 years ago, and Burmese Buddhists revere it as their most beautiful pilgrimage center. It contains eight sacred relics given by the Buddha to two Burmese followers. Fine carvings, statues, and mosaics are found in the more than eighty-two shrines at the many levels that encircle the immense central *stupa,* or shrine, which contains the Buddha relics. The Prayer Pavilion alone has twenty-eight statues of Buddha.

• Sri Pada, Sri Lanka

An ancient name for Sri Lanka is *serendip,* from which comes the term "serendipity," which means to find something important while searching for something else. Thousands of pilgrims who make their way up this holy mountain, Sri Pada, would agree that serendipity is precisely what happens as they climb. They are in search of a sacred footprint said to be located at the first place Buddha stood on earth. (The name for the mountain itself comes from *pada,* meaning "footprint," and *sri,* a term of respect.) Buddhist pilgrims travel to the top each year with their families, including children and grandparents. They discover on the way the importance of their familial ties and the sacredness of their own life together.

• Stonehenge, England

Probably the best-known prehistoric monument in Britain, Stonehenge ranks as one of the most powerfully spiritual sites in Europe. It consists of a series of giant stones, and may have been used both as a site for religious ceremonies and as an observatory for predicting solstices and eclipses. Contemporary pagans, New-Agers, and druids seek to celebrate their spirituality here.

• Taizé, France

In 1940, a French-Swiss monk named Brother Roger founded an ecumenical Christian community in the village of Taizé, and it has become one of the most popular pilgrimage sites in Europe. Pope John XXIII referred to it as "that little springtime." Young people especially are drawn to it for its emphasis on Christian unity, its non-dogmatic approach, its beautiful liturgies, and its educational workshops and discussions. Community members come from different ecclesial traditions and yet pray and minister together. Many monks leave Taizé to work in the poorest parts of Africa, Asia, and the Americas.

• Tours, France

This city became an important center of Christianity in the fourth century under St. Martin, bishop of Tours. As his fame spread, Tours became a major pilgrimage site; a gigantic church was built to house his tomb and relics. Several popes have gone to this church as pilgrims, including Urban II, John XXIII, and John Paul II. During the French Revolution, the church was partially demolished. Another basilica was built near the original site; it is visited by thousands of people today.

Vatican City

St. Peter's Basilica, the largest Catholic church anywhere, is situated in the independent sovereign state, Vatican City, in the middle of Rome. It is considered the main church of Roman Catholicism and of the pope. The first church on this site was constructed in 323 by the Emperor Constantine. Over a thousand years later, Pope Nicholas V conceived a plan to level the old church and build a new one, and to finance the project through the sale of indulgences. This set in motion the dissent of Martin Luther and the beginning of the Protestant Reformation. Today millions of people of all beliefs visit this grand structure to pray in community with others and to stand in awe at the artistic and architectural wonders it contains.

Vézalay, France

The historic abbey church of Sainte-Madeleine [Mary Magdalene] at Vézalay is one of the wonders of medieval art. According to medieval stories, Mary had left the Holy Land and traveled to Provence, where she became a hermit and lived in a cave at Saint-Baume, not far from Aix. During the ninth century, however, pilgrims associated her with Vézalay, and, after rumors placed her bodily relics there, in 1120 construction of the beautiful romanesque church began. Vézalay was on one of the four roads pilgrims followed from France to the shrine at Santiago de Compostela. St. Bernard of Clairvaux preached there, and the second and third crusades were launched there. Today Mary Magdalene's church continues to attract pilgrims because of its historical significance and artistic beauty.

• Walsingham, England

In the middle ages, Walsingham, near the north coast of Norfolk, was second only to Canterbury as England's greatest pilgrimage site. The shrine contained "the Holy House," which supposedly was modeled on the house in which Jesus' mother had lived. The English Reformation, under Henry VIII, closed and destroyed most of it, but in the late nineteenth century a revival of pilgrimage there began. Pilgrims of all faiths, especially Roman Catholic and Anglican Christians, now gather there.

Westminster Abbey, England

This abbey is closely linked with the history of England. It contains the tombs of numerous political leaders, such as Edward the Confessor (1003–1066) and Queen Elizabeth I, along with poets and writers from Chaucer to T. S. Eliot. The abbey occupies the site of an earlier shrine, built by Edward the Confessor, which had become a pilgrimage site. Westminster Abbey is one of the most popular holy sites in London.

A Doable Pilgrimage

Often travel to the best known pilgrimage destinations involves great distance and significant expense. Many people may never get the opportunity to go to such a site, or the chance may only come once in a lifetime. But that doesn't mean you can't go on a pilgrimage. Some ideas to pursue in order to experience a doable pilgrimage:

- Choose a site or place nearer to home that you perhaps have overlooked—or possibly have always wanted to visit, but never made time for.

- Consult your immediate family or relatives about sites associated with your ancestors, maybe locations where they lived or cemeteries where they lie buried; listen for stories which may link you more closely with them—and your own heritage and identity.

- If possible, check on the internet for more information about the site and its landscape, and how to get there.

- Read about its history or, if linked with your family inheritance, search for any recorded information, including writings, letters, or journals that family members might have in their possession; if you have time, trace your genealogy.

- Set aside a week or weekend or, if that's not possible, a day which will allow you to travel to such sites, and spend some time visiting unhurriedly.

- If you intend to go alone, take some writing paper along with which to journal, describing what you see and its effect on you emotionally, psychologically, spiritually.

- If you want to have companions on the road, ask family members or friends if they might be interested in making the journey with you.

- While traveling, take time to listen to music that will encourage reflection and contemplation.

- Give yourself enough time at the site or cemetery to deepen your awareness of what you see; look for local guides who know the place and who can help you communicate with the past; take photographs, light candles, pray.

- At the conclusion of your pilgrimage, celebrate your pilgrimage with some form of ritual, and, if companions have accompanied you, plan a meal to commemorate your experience, encouraging participants to tell their stories of what they saw and experienced.

What every pilgrim needs to practice

- the discipline of mindfulness: paying attention, listening, living in the moment
- the discipline of daily prayer upon rising and before sleeping
- the discipline of reading sacred texts before leaving on pilgrimage, during one's travels, and after one's return
- the discipline of asking questions, seeking direction
- the discipline of journaling or of quiet reflection
- the discipline of letting go, being open to the mystery
- the discipline of gratitude for all one sees, and all one meets

Top Ten Books on Pilgrimage

Calamari, Barbara, and Sandra DiPasqua. *Holy Places: Sacred Sites in Catholicism.* New York: Viking Studio, 2002.

Coleman, Simon, and John Elsner. *Pilgrimage: Past and Present in the World Religions.* Cambridge: Harvard University Press, 1995.

Cousineau, Phil. *The Art of Pilgrimage: The Seeker's Guide to Making Travel Sacred.* Berkeley, CA: Conari Press, 1998.

Harpur, James. *Sacred Tracks: 2000 Years of Christian Pilgrimage.* Berkeley, CA: University of California Press, 2002.

Mahoney, Rosemary. *The Singular Pilgrim: Travels on Sacred Ground.* Boston: Houghton Mifflin Co., 2003.

Pentkovsky, Aleksei, ed. *The Pilgrim's Tale*. New York: Paulist Press, 1999.

Robinson, Martin. *Sacred Places, Pilgrim Paths: An Anthology of Pilgrimage*. New York: HarperCollins, 1995.

Sumption, Jonathan. *Pilgrimage: An Image of Medieval Religion*. Totowa, NJ: Rowman and Littlefield, 1976.

Turner, Victor, and Edith Turner. *Image and Pilgrimage in Christian Culture*. New York: Columbia Press, 1978.

Westwood, Jennifer. *On Pilgrimage: Sacred Journeys Around the World*. Mahwah, NJ: HiddenSpring, 2003.

Five Pilgrimage Classics

Canterbury Tales—In Geoffrey Chaucer's staple of western literature we meet every man and woman in a storytelling competition as they travel to pay homage to St. Thomas Becket at Canterbury.

Pilgrim's Progress—Writing from his prison cell, John Bunyan's allegory portrays our spiritual journey from the first encounter with the spirit to the gates of heaven, from the "City of Destruction" to the "Celestial City."

The Way of a Pilgrim—This classic of eastern Christianity follows an Orthodox monk as he visits monasteries from Russia to Siberia in an effort to follow St. Paul's instruction to "pray without ceasing."

Piers The Plowman—Set in fourteenth century England, this spiritual allegory explores the meaning of life in relation to our ultimate purpose.

The Path To Rome—Hillaire Belloc walks across Europe to the Eternal City before the twentieth century's world wars changed it irrevocably.

Five Contemporary Pilgrimage Classics

Pilgrimage—Bestselling Brazilian author Paulo Coehlo recounts his journey along the Camino de Compostela, a book that helped reinvigorate contemporary Camino pilgrimages.

Siddhartha—Perhaps Hermann Hesse's best known work, this novel tells the story of a young man's quest for the contemplative life and spiritual wisdom.

Seven Storey Mountain—Thomas Merton tells of his journey from a thoroughly secular world to the Trappist monastery at Gethsemani.

Snow Leopard—Author Peter Matthiessen's search for the elusive and beautiful snow leopard in the Himalayas becomes a spiritual quest and an unfolding of his inner self.

Arctic Dreams—Naturalist author Barry Lopez examines the world of the arctic and evolves an understanding of the spirituality of place.

Five Great Pilgrimage Movies

Wild Strawberries—Ingmar Bergman's emotional tale of a man who reviews his life while driving to receive an honorary degree.

2001: A Space Odyssey—Stanley Kubrick's masterpiece about the human desire to connect with other life in the universe.

Meetings with A Remarkable Man—Chronicles cult leader A.J. Gurdjieff's journey through Asia in search of the meaning of life.

Lawrence of Arabia—Masterful portrayal of the life of British adventurer T.E. Lawrence, based on his book *The Seven Pillars of Wisdom.*

Field of Dreams—Baseball, the great American metaphor, is the vehicle for this magical tale of hope and redemption.

A Select Bibliography on Pilgrimage

Adams, Henry. *Mont Saint Michel and Chartres.* New York: Penguin Books, 1986.

Basho, Matsuo. *Narrow Road to the Interior and Other Writings.* Boston: Shambhala, 1998.

Beston, Henry. *The Outermost House: A Year of Life on the Great Beach of Cape Cod.* New York: Henry Holt and Co., 1988.

Bird, Isabella. *Six Months in the Sandwich Islands.* Honolulu: Mutual Publishing, 2001.

Burton, Naomi, Br. Patrick Hart, and James Laughlin, eds. *The Asian Journal of Thomas Merton.* New York: New Directions Books, 1973.

Calamari, Barbara, and Sandra DiPasqua. *Holy Places: Sacred Sites in Catholicism.* New York: Viking Studio, 2002.

Clift, Jean, and Wallace B. Clift. *The Archetype of Pilgrimage: Outer Action With Inner Meaning*. New York: Paulist Press, 1996.

Coleman, Simon, and John Elsner. *Pilgrimage: Past and Present in the World Religions*. Cambridge, MA: Harvard University Press, 1995.

Cousineau, Phil. *The Art of Pilgrimage: The Seeker's Guide to Making Travel Sacred*. Berkeley, CA: Conari Press, 1998.

Culligan, M., and P. Cherici. *The Wandering Irish in Europe*. London: Constable, 2000.

De Custine, Astolphe. *Letters from Russia*. New York: New York Review of Books, 2002.

Du Boulay, Shirley. *The Road to Canterbury: A Modern Pilgrimage*. London: HarperCollins, 1994.

Duckett, Eleanor. *The Wandering Saints*. London: Catholic Book Club, 1960.

Eliot, T. S. *Four Quartets*. New York: Harcourt Brace Jovanovich, 1971.

Fermor, Patrick Leigh. *A Time to Keep Silence*. Pleasantville, NY: The Akadine Press, 1997.

Forest, Jim. *Pilgrim to the Russian Church.* New York: Crossroad, 1988.

French, R. M., trans. *The Way of a Pilgrim and The Pilgrim Continues His Way.* HarperSanFrancisco, 1991.

Galland, China. *Longing for Darkness: Tara and the Black Madonna.* New York: Penguin Books, 1990.

Green, Hannah. *Little Saint.* New York: Random House, 2000.

Hager, June. *Pilgrimage: A Chronicle of Christianity Through the Churches of Rome.* London: Weidenfeld & Nicolson, 1999.

Hampl, Patricia. *Virgin Time: In Search of the Contemplative Life.* New York: Ballantine Books, 1992.

Harpur, James. *Sacred Tracks: 2000 Years of Christian Pilgrimage.* Berkeley, CA: University of California Press, 2002.

Harrison, Peter. *Pilgrimage in Ireland.* Syracuse, NY: University of Syracuse Press, 1992.

Heath, Sidney. *Pilgrim Life in the Middle Ages.* Boston: Houghton Mifflin Co., 1912.

Jones, Andrew. *Every Pilgrim's Guide to Celtic Britain and Ireland*. Liguori, MO: Liguori Publications, 2002.

Kerouac, Jack. *On the Road*. New York: Penguin Books, 1955.

________. *The Dharma Bums*. New York: Penguin Books, 1958.

Langland, William. *Piers the Ploughman*. New York: Penguin, 1986.

Mahoney, Rosemary. *The Singular Pilgrim: Travels on Sacred Ground*. Boston: Houghton Mifflin Co., 2003.

May, Rollo. *My Quest for Beauty*. San Francisco: Saybrook, 1985.

McPherson, Anne. *Walking to the Saints: A Little Pilgrimage in France*. New York: Paulist Press, 2000.

Merton, Thomas. *Mystics and Zen Masters*. New York: Noonday Press, 1967.

Miller, Malcolm. *Chartres Cathedral*. Norwich, England: Jarrold Publishing, 1996.

Munro, Eleanor. *On Glory Roads: A Pilgrim's Book About Pilgrimage*. London: Thames & Hudson, 1987.

Ni Mheara, Roisin. *Early Irish Saints in Europe: Their Sites and Their Stories.* Armagh, No. Ireland: Armagh Diocesan Historical Society, 2001.

Palmer, Martin, and Nigel Palmer. *England, Scotland, Wales: The Guide to Sacred Sites and Pilgrim Routes in Britain.* Mahwah, NJ: HiddenSpring, 2000.

Robinson, Martin. *Sacred Places, Pilgrim Paths: An Anthology of Pilgrimage.* New York: HarperCollins, 1995.

Roy, James Charles. *The Back of Beyond: A Search for the Soul of Ireland.* Cambridge: Westview Press, 2002.

Stevenson, Robert Louis. *Travels in Hawaii.* Honolulu: University of Hawaii Press, 1991.

Sumption, Jonathan. *Pilgrimage: An Image of Medieval Religion.* Totowa, NJ: Rowman and Littlefield, 1976.

Tolstoy, Leo. "Two Old Men," in *Walk in the Light and Twenty-three Tales.* Farmington, PA: Plough Publishing House, 1998.

Turner, Victor, and Edith Turner. *Image and Pilgrimage in Christian Culture.* New York: Columbia Press, 1978.

Vest, Douglas. *On Pilgrimage.* Cambridge, MA: Cowley, 1998.

Waddell, Helen. *The Wandering Scholars.* Ann Arbor, MI: University of Michigan Press, 1992.

Westwood, Jennifer. *On Pilgrimage: Sacred Journeys Around the World.* Mahwah, NJ: HiddenSpring, 2003.

Whyte, David. *Crossing the Unknown Sea: Work as a Pilgrimage of Identity.* NY: Riverhead Books, 2001.

Wilson, Colin. *The Atlas of Holy Places and Sacred Sites.* London: Dorling Kindersley Ltd., 1996.

Edward C. Sellner, Ph.D., is professor of pastoral theology and spirituality at the College of St. Catherine in St. Paul, Minnesota. He is the author of numerous articles and books, including *Wisdom of the Celtic Saints* and *The Celtic Soul Friend,* and most recently, *Stories of the Celtic Soul Friends: Their Meaning for Today.* A popular speaker on Celtic spirituality, he has given workshops, retreats, and lectures at local, national, and international conferences and leads pilgrimages to the holy places of the Celtic saints in Ireland, Brittany, Cornwall, and Galicia in Spain.